YOU CAN,
END OF STORY

CORY LEWIS

BALBOA.
PRESS
A DIVISION OF HAY HOUSE

Balboa Press books may be ordered through booksellers or by contacting:

Balboa Press
A Division of Hay House
1663 Liberty Drive
Bloomington, IN 47403
www.balboapress.com
1 (877) 407-4847

Because of the dynamic nature of the Internet, any web addresses or
links contained in this book may have changed since publication and
may no longer be valid. The views expressed in this work are solely those
of the author and do not necessarily reflect the views of the publisher,
and the publisher hereby disclaims any responsibility for them.

The author of this book does not dispense medical advice or prescribe the use
of any technique as a form of treatment for physical, emotional, or medical
problems without the advice of a physician, either directly or indirectly. The
intent of the author is only to offer information of a general nature to help
you in your quest for emotional and spiritual well-being. In the event you use
any of the information in this book for yourself, which is your constitutional
right, the author and the publisher assume no responsibility for your actions.

Any people depicted in stock imagery provided by Thinkstock are
models, and such images are being used for illustrative purposes only.
Certain stock imagery © Thinkstock.

Print information available on the last page.

ISBN: 978-1-5043-7647-1 (sc)
ISBN: 978-1-5043-7648-8 (e)

Balboa Press rev. date: 09/30/2019

This book is dedicated to my three daughters who, consistently inspire me to keep dreaming and being my best everyday, I love you with all my heart, Milan, Na'ima and Mia. To my lovely wife Merlene, I am so happy you are in my life, you're more than a mother and wife, you're also my best friend and partner.

May God continue to Bless you all and may we be a blessing and example to others. To God be the Glory Forever and ever, Amen.

CONTENTS

Preface

THIS BOOK IS DESIGNED to Wake **YOU** Up! If you're feeling a little off course, like you tried everything and are not where you want to be, in your life, career, marriage, whatever it may be, then keep reading. The power of "You Can" is still within you, and it's not too late to reactivate that power! I don't care if you just learned to read or are 100 years old, these principles apply to you right now, and it's time you tapped into your hidden ideas, and gifts you were born with, your natural God given talents. My goal is to get you feeling like you can run through a brick wall after reading this book, like the Superman/Superwoman you are! Let's get you pumped up and excited about life again, starting now!

CHAPTER

What Happened?

THINK BACK TO WHEN you were five years old, what did you want to be? A Doctor, Astronaut, a Professional Football Player, a Pilot, maybe a Superhero? I wanted to be Superman more than anything in the world. My daughter at age 5 said after she saw President Obama become President she wanted to become President of the United States. She would run around the house saying one day she would become president. She was so excited, and I encouraged her to the fullest. I told her she could be anything she wanted, however two years later I asked her what she wanted to be when she grew up and she said an Actor, or Singer. I thought to myself, What Happened? I thought, how could she want to lower her goal from President of the United States to an Actress or Singer? I didn't understand it all, however maybe that is what happens to all of us in our life. When we are children our imagination is so open, that we feel unstoppable like a superhero. Our minds and hearts are filled with unlimited potential, however our interpersonal relationships, environment we grow up in and things we go through on a daily basis shape and conform our minds into settling for less than our best. Maybe you had a rough childhood, your parents weren't there for you the way you thought they should have been or you had no one to look up too, no mentor or guidance. There is a divine reason why you picked up this book and are reading it right now. I am a strong believer that nothing in our vast universe happens by mistake. You are in the right place at the right time for your life, it's not too late to reestablish those dreams and goals. What happened to your dreams? They are still there within you, and if it were easy, everyone would be doing it. This book is a fire starter and I will be frank with you, in order to motivate you into the person I know you really are. No matter what you did yesterday or how many times you have failed doesn't matter anymore. There is an old Chinese proverb that says, "Fall down seven times, stand up eight". You must stand up after the loss, after the disappointment. You may have fallen down but don't stay down. Life is just like being in a boxing match, you will get hit. You get hit with sickness, you get hit by losing your job, you get hit by losing a loved one, you get hit with loneliness, depression, What happened? Life Happened. None of us are immune to these life events that knock us down, and force us to think differently about our personal goals and aspirations, but how you respond will make all the difference. Life is ten percent of what happens to you and ninety percent how you deal with it. Ask yourself, "What do I want?" What is it, that you have been holding onto, that dream that you just can't seem to let go of? Were you planning on starting a business, writing a book, scoring a film? There is something that you know you are supposed to do, and you're not doing it. Was it losing weight, or asking that special someone out on a date? Whatever it is, take some time, close your eyes and say to yourself, "What do I want?", meditate on it, pray over it, fast, and ask to be lead in the right direction I guarantee once you meditate and sleep on it, your brain will get to work with ideas and solutions. The magnificent thing about you is that even when you're sleeping, your brain is still active. I recall many times going to sleep and waking up the very next day with so many ideas and plans, I was ready to conquer the day! I am sure that has happened to you as well. If you fail to plan, you plan to fail. You have the power within you to activate, your dream thoughts into reality, but it takes an action plan. You can't be lazy with this either! Your mindset cannot be some lazy, wishy washy hazy wave particle. It either Is or it Isn't, there is no in between. The great Yoda, once said, "Do or Do not, there is no try." This mean you have to make a decision to be successful, you must decide to be great, you must be certain without any doubts and claim your victories even before they happen. I do enjoy listening to Eric Thomas and Les Brown, just Google those names and listen to what they have to say I promise you, you will be motivated beyond measure! Open your heart and mind, to be able to listen to your inner thoughts. Ask yourself, "What is my passion?" "What do I love to do?" "What do I do better than anyone else?". Once you know what that is, the next question to ask yourself is, "Who is going to pay me to do what I love?" Your passion can become your purpose, your career. The next thing you should do is create your action plan. It should consist of a 30, 60, 90 day plan followed by a one-year plan, five-year plan and 10 year plan. You must do something intentional every single day that gets you a little closer to your goal. This will take discipline, you must be disciplined as you are in the planning stage. Remember to get plenty of rest, eat clean foods, try to eat food that is good for you not just good in taste. Who doesn't like to eat a double from In and Out every once in a while, I know I do. Try to get at least 30 minutes of exercise in daily go for a walk, go to the gym do something to get you active. Take time to be alone go by yourself somewhere for 10 minutes a day just to meditate and be alone with your thoughts. When you do these things you alleviate the stress from your life and allow your mind to become more focused and your energy better directed. I recall when I was 18 I met Russell Simons in Macy's at the Fox Hills Mall in Los Angeles at one of his clothing launches. I'll never forget what he told me, he said, "Always have balance in your life." I never really understood what that meant until I got a little older. What he was trying to tell me was that I needed order to remember to keep things in perspective, there is a time for work and there's a time for play, there is a time for rest and a time to create. I guess he could tell that even back then I was kind of all over the place I just graduated and I didn't know what I wanted to do with my life as most 18 year olds are. I thank God that I never was a drinker and never wanted to do drugs so I never joined that crowd. I just wanted to make something of myself so I started writing songs. I loved R&B music and still do, so my first years of college I took every music class I could. I took song writing 101, commercial song writing, music production, piano, recording techniques and sampling. My plan was to be the best songwriter I could be and turn that passion into money. I did that for many years, but found that what I really enjoyed more than making music was selling music. I learned that one of my talents, was selling and I am very good at it. We are all good at something, you have talent and you know exactly what it is. The confusion lies within what you think you want and what you actually want deep down. Once you arrive at the truth, you will have come home spiritually. From that you will find the meaning of life, more specifically your life and what you were created to do. People search there entire life looking for their meaning, or purpose. Why not start by helping others? There is a saying, "If you help people get what they want, eventually you will get what you want." I believe this to be very true, when you help your boss at work, you develop trust, and he will see you as a leader. Remember the more people you help, the easier it will be for people to help you. Maybe you're a shy person, you keep an emotional distance away from people? A good thing to do is start to include yourself socially, attend that church gathering, go to the block party, seek people out, knowing people is almost as good as cash in the bank. How many times have you gotten an opportunity simply because you knew someone, a friend, a co-worker, family? You might even call it a hook up, but the fact is we all have been hooked up just because we knew someone on the inside of the place we wanted to be. That's how it works, when you help someone that favor, that blessing, will be coming back to you tenfold! It may not happen today or tomorrow but trust and believe that it is on the way. Maybe you feel like you have helped everyone around you and no one cares. Never forget there is always someone taking notes, keeping track, and seeing what you do daily. Your good work will not go unnoticed forever, and when you stop thinking about it, when you least expect it, BOOM! Here comes the gift, the blessings, the favor you dreamed of. Keep being the good person you are, show up to work, school, church, early, be kind and get to know the people around you, don't be afraid to include yourself. Ever heard the saying, "Scared money don't, make money". Remember that you are more valuable than money, your words are like cash, and the way you carry yourself adds value to you! Don't be cheap and give your time to cheap things that add zero value to yourself. People will pull on you and try to hold you back. They want you in the same boat as them, my advice to you is, don't let them. Develop order, Develop strength, now you're ready to begin.

CHAPTER

Start Saying YES!

WHEN SOMEONE SAYS No to you, how do you feel? rejected, hurt. When the bank says, you're not approved, or when you're at the register making that purchase and the person says, you're card is declined! I guess that has only happened to me, how do you feel? Like you want to run and hide! It's like they are saying you're not good enough to have this or buy that. The fact is most people today are credit challenged maybe you've made a lot of mistakes in your past that to this very day are still on your credit report. Why not go to www.annualcreditreport. com and dispute everything that is on your report? What amazes me the most is that people tell me their dreams, their thoughts, their goals, all the things that they wish to accomplish but never get started. In essence they are saying no to themselves they are saying no to their dreams they are saying no to their hopes and aspirations. Whoever told you couldn't accomplish your dreams, you need to say no to them you need to say no to their negativity you do not need that in your life. By nature I am a very competitive person, I hate to lose, I've been that way my entire life growing up in a family that would play basketball every weekend. I will never forget one Saturday afternoon I was at Cheviot Hills Park in West Los Angeles playing basketball with my two older brothers Cliff and Sheldon, when the "R.Kelly" pulls up with an entire basketball team entourage with him. I was amazed he actually brought a bunch of 7 foot guys with him to ensure that he would not lose a single game I thought to myself, this guy came to win! Not only did his team win, they dominated. They only left the court when they were tired of winning. I learned a valuable lesson that day when you prepare and you plan to win, you win. R. Kelly knew what he was doing, he surrounded himself with the best team and that was the reason he won. Who are you surrounding yourself with today are they winners or losers, successes or failures? You can lessen the likelihood of you hearing the words no by surrounding yourself with the best team, no not the best friends the best team. If you are the smartest person amongst your friends you need new friends. Look at your friends today, no really look at the friends you have right now most of them you probably don't need at all but you keep them around you for sentimental reasons maybe you grew up with them, knew them your entire life and have grown up being with them all the time. Are they the people that tell you no or yes? Do they build you up? Do they add value to your life? Do they help you when you need them? After I graduated high school I had a lot of cutting to do a lot of friends to delete. I could see the path that they were going on and I did not like it. You have to be strong enough to end unhealthy relationships. You cannot be afraid of what other people think or other people say, this is your life you're in charge you make decisions, all the decisions. Are your friends more interested in going out to the clubs, bars, staying out late every night while you are more focused on your work, your business and becoming successful? Birds of a feather flock together, but what kind of bird are you? Have you ever noticed that Chickens and Eagles do not hang out together? One is designed to stay on the ground and be eaten, you know "Kentucky fried chicken". Have you ever had eagle fried chicken? I doubt it. That is because one bird was designed to be consumed/eaten while the other bird was designed to fly high above all the rest, which one are you? The chicken gets told no I'm going to eat you, I'm going to turn you into chicken noodle soup, I'm going to fry you, I'm going to shred you and make enchiladas. Don't have the chicken mentality, have the eagle mentality. Start saying yes to yourself, yes to your dreams, yes to your hopes, yes to your blessings, yes to your favor. Too many times we get discouraged when we lose in life and we start telling ourselves no. We have to get in the habit of approving ourselves! No matter what you credit looks like no matter how in debt you are start by saying today's a new day and I will tell myself yes.

— 9 —

Yes to promotion, yes to growth, yes all day long. When you start doing this, the universe has no choice but to move out of your way, start today. It's very easy for us to get comfortable right where we are with the relationship that were in, the job that we have, the money that we make, the car that we drive, the school we attend, the church that we go to even the grocery store are all habits. We go to the places we are most comfortable with, we are creatures of habit. Even the uncomfortable relationships we sometimes choose to stay in even if they are physically abusive, or verbally abusive we must be strong enough to step away from all of those. You were not created to be hurt, you were created to have joy in all aspects of your life however you are in charge of your own happiness. No one else can make you happy, not your friends, not your spouse, not your coworkers, not your family. Don't depend or wait for anyone to bring happiness to your life. How do you wake up in the morning? You should wake up full of joy telling yourself today will be a great day, today I will conquer all things thrown my way, nothing will stop me! If you wake up with this type of attitude you're destined to have a wonderful day. Too often we wake up just the opposite saying to ourselves is it Monday again? Today I have to face the boss it will be horrible lousy no good very bad day. The reality is too many times we wake up with those thoughts and feelings. It's time for you to switch it up! Get up a little earlier tomorrow your goal should be every morning wake up before the alarm clock goes off. It may sound like a small thing but every time you wake up before the alarm clock goes off you just created a small accomplishment for yourself. When you wake up in the morning the first words that you say to yourself are very powerful remember words have creative power so if the first thing that you say to yourself is positive then you will have a positive day and the opposite is very true. You set the expectation for the day in your mind even before you leave the house. You are in effect telling the universe today is my day, it will be a great day nothing will get in my way, I will leave and return home safely to my loved ones and I will be a blessing and I will be blessed today. When you speak these powerful affirmations you will see things come true right before your very eyes. There is no competition in fact the only competition is yourself don't limit yourself. You are limitless, and unstoppable. Never forget the world was created with the power of words as did God in the beginning. He said, "Let there be light, and there was light." Remember you are created in the image of God, therefore your words have a special creative power. Never talk bad about yourself! I hear so many people say, the words, "I am so stupid." Why anyone would ever say that about themselves is beyond my understanding. Is that what you really think about yourself, or did you just make a mistake? Never, ever degrade or speak negativity over your life. The words you say about yourself are like a magnet they can draw good things or bad things. I know many people who have cancer and who are sick, truly sick. I know many people who have gout and many others who have aches and pains many people who can barely walk. Remember to speak healing over your body over yourself since your words create worlds create a world for yourself that is full complete and whole. You might be in pain right now but don't speak about it, don't admit it. Instead train your mind to have a new attitude, you might be truly sick but say to yourself, I am healed, I am not hurting, I feel good. Even if none of that is true at the moment there has been many case studies that have been done that show when you speak good things about yourself your brain goes to work and starts to release the energy that you need. Change things around start telling yourself how smart you are, how beautiful you are, how thin you are, how athletic you are, how talented you are, how generous you are. Remember that you are more than a champion, you're more than victorious, you're more than a winner and that everything you need to accomplish your goals is already inside of you, screaming to be released into the world. Stay away from all forms of negativity, negative people and negative thoughts they will do nothing but bring you down to their level the chicken level. Remember that is not where you belong you are an eagle destined to fly. You no longer have time or energy to waste with people who do not share your vision or your passion about life. Your time is limited so you need to start now and anyone who does not understand that needs to move out of your way. Today's the day, not yesterday not tomorrow but today the day, not yesterday not tomorrow but today. You will rejoice and have joy today you will say yes to your dreams and everything you hope for will come to you. It doesn't matter if no one ever gives you the complements or praise. You can do that yourself when you get up in the morning look in the mirror and say to yourself good morning you beautiful thing you wonderful creation. The point of this is simple, you have to start feeling good you have to start feeling better about yourself. Never doubt yourself, never let your mind wander thinking about what if's. Be certain and intentional in everything that you do when you're getting ready to walk outside of the door in the morning put on nice clothes, groom yourself the best you can because every day whether you realize it or not someone is watching you. Someone is watching what time you arrive at work, at school, at church. Believe it or not there's always someone who wishes they had your life, who wishes they had your car, who wishes they had your job, who wishes they had your husband or wife. Start saying yes to your future to your dreams to your goals. I'm sure you've been around plenty of negative people already and being around them will only allow their spirit to rub off on you. Many people are bitter for whatever reason they feel like they missed out like they never received what they truly deserved. Many people feel entitled like someone owes them something. We must do our best to stay away from these feelings and people. Some of these people may even be some of your own family and that's fine, we all have the ability to love our family members from a distance. I have learned to do that with many of my family members. I love them, but I don't love the way they live their life and because of that we have nothing in common other than our family relationship. You have to be able to distinguish what you want and which people will help you get there. You know what you want in life and you know what it takes to get there say, "Yes" to it.

CHAPTER

Everyday Opportunity

WE NEVER KNOW WHAT'S going to happen one moment from the next, life is so unpredictable. I recall a time where I was at home and I got a phone call from a very good friend of mine he said hey my uncle is in town for the next couple of days and I'd like you to meet him, I thought to myself sure, I'll tag along. We end up taking a drive to the Four Seasons Hotel we go up to the top floor and I see a bodyguard standing in front of the door he asked who we are and he pats us down then he proceeds to let us into the room. We walk into the room and in the left corner of the room I see a man wearing a gold colored suit with shiny black boots with pink flowers on them, it was none other than the Godfather of Rock 'n' Roll, Little Richard. I was in complete shock! This man defined a generation & created timeless legendary music, and now I am sitting less than 1 foot away from him, talk about pressure. Little Richard was extremely friendly and we went want to talk for hours about his life and legacy in music. He told me that Michael Jackson would call him often and ask him for business advice & he also gave advice to Prince, Usher and any other artists that needed help. He spoke about how he gave all of them relationship advice and while it would not be appropriate to say exactly what he said, he basically told them to watch out for women who would be only interested in them for financial gain. Little Richard then asked us if we were hungry and after spending about three hours with him we were, so he decided to order room service and he ordered us the most expensive tuna fish sandwich and french fries I had ever eaten. The final bill was about $500, however that is his mere pocket change when you're the Godfather of Rock 'n' Roll music. We spoke about life and we spoke about opportunities Little Richard said, to use your opportunities wisely and really think about what it is that you want out of life. Do you want to continue to do music and write songs? If so what steps have you taken to make your dreams come true? Then he asked me to sing for him, talk about being nervous. Here is a man that is sold millions of albums worldwide a wonderful talented musician. After I pick my stomach up off of the floor I sang out the best notes that I thought I could and afterward he said you have talent don't waste it create your opportunities then you will be successful. Talk about a mind blowing experience here I was just a few hours ago sitting at home, now I'm sitting in front of and just sang for one of the greatest musicians in all of history. I was so humbled, and thankful that I got to meet him and spend a little bit of time with him. It really showed me that this is how life is one moment you're at home, the next you get a call, then you're in a place that you never knew you would be in, but what you do after that is up to you. The world famous martial artist and actor Bruce Lee, once said, "Forget your circumstances create your opportunities". How many of you were doing that today? Not looking at where you came from or what you did in the past but truly focused on what you want now. All the creative power you need is in you, but sitting on the couch instead of brainstorming ideas will put you back months, sometimes maybe even years. That one day that you did nothing productive can completely throw you off course. Get out a pen and paper and start formulating your game plan, your opportunities. Who enjoys waiting? That's one of the things that I'm constantly working on is my patience. I don't like waiting in long lines in fact for this reason I barely go to Costco to get gas. I do not like the long lines at Disneyland or any amusement park, they make me not want to go at all. I really need to work on my patience. Imagine how far along you would be if you were impatient for your goals and your dreams, you couldn't wait for them, you couldn't wait to get up in the morning to start your day, you couldn't wait to get to work on your next project you couldn't wait to get started, I think that would be a good thing. Every day is a fresh 24 hours to make something happen. We all have the same amount of hours in a day, the same amount of seconds, but what we don't have is the same opportunities. How will you capitalize on your opportunities today? What are you going to do differently that is going to set your idea your plan apart from everyone and everything else that is out there? What are you going to do that's going to make a difference in your life and in others? Maybe you had an opportunity years ago to do something really great but you let fear take over and you never capitalized on the opportunity you let it slip away. The good news is there will always be more there'll always be another chance but you have to recognize when it's there. When I met my wife I was already tied up in a relationship, I had a girlfriend. However I could feel in my spirit that the girlfriend that I was with was not the right person for me I could feel it so deeply inside every day. I knew she was not the girl for me, I knew that I could never see myself marrying this person so I had to ask myself why is she my girlfriend? The purpose of dating someone is to someday marry them but if I did not have that intention, I knew it was time for me to let her go. How selfish of me would I be to hold onto someone that I knew I did not want in my life. Are you doing that today? Are you holding up your own opportunity or someone else's? If you are, let them go, free yourself, free that other person don't waste their time and don't waste yours. You have the power not only to create opportunities for yourself but also for others and life is too short to miss out on every day opportunities. When I met my wife Merlene, we were working for the same company in Carson. I thought to myself who is this beautiful girl, and what attracted me the most to her was her innocence her personality and joy. Too many of the women around me at that time had attitudes, bitterness bad previous relationships that they would constantly talk about. That is definitely one way to scare a man off, by carrying on the previous drama to the next relationship. I say this very respectfully but ladies, if you start a relationship with a new man recognize he is a new man give him a chance and if he is good to you, be good to him but don't carry the hurt, the guilt, the pain, the frustration to him because he will not stay around long if you do. Give him a fresh opportunity and he will give you a fresh opportunity every day. No relationship is perfect as 50% of marriages end in divorce. Maybe you came from one of those homes that ended up in divorce? I am here to tell you that it does not matter what your mom did, or what your dad did. You have an opportunity to have a wonderful relationship with the person that you truly love. Maybe you didn't see or experience that growing up but it doesn't matter though. You can make it better for yourself and for your children before the next generation by showing love to others and redefining what true love really is. Life is not a fairytale there are no Prince Charming's and there are no Kings or Queens. Disney would like you to think otherwise, every single movie that they make involves some sort of Prince or Princess, some sort of kingdom, some sort of castle, some sort of fairytale reality that none of us actually ever experience, why is that? Maybe it's because they're trying to sell us something, the idea of a perfect world full of peace and harmony. They are very good at it, their movies and TV shows gross billions of dollars for them every single year. So maybe the idea of a happy ending intrigues the minds of many, an idea where the guy gets the girl and they ride off into the sunset together. There amusement park fittingly is called the happiest place on earth. They know that people have a need or desire to feel happy, to be happy, to have joy in their life. People pay year after year to attend this place to feel this joy, this happiness with their loved ones, their families. The idea of Disneyland was brilliant from the very start they realized that happiness is an everyday opportunity and they realize that people would pay almost anything to experience it. So they sell us a $100 admission ticket, a $10 bag of popcorn, a $10 turkey leg, a $5 balloon and we buy it all, we pay the price every time. You Can be the next Walt Disney! What do people want that you can create or offer? Happiness? Love? Peace? Guidance? Create your Opportunity.

CHAPTER

4

Your Inner Greatness

You may be thinking, I am not much good, let alone great at anything. Maybe you weren't much of an athlete, couldn't sing to save your life, wasn't the best student in school. The great news is none of that matters to the person you are right now. I guarantee in your life, someone has come up to you and attempted to pull out your inner greatness. A few months ago I was walking through a Target store and this little old lady came up to me and tugged on my shirt, and she looked me in the eye and said "Hello Pastor". I told her, "I am sorry, I am not a Pastor, I am a Deacon and I do attend church with my family regularly." She looked at me up and down and said, "No you're a Pastor, not a Bishop, but a Pastor." I thought to myself is this lady crazy, or is she speaking a prophesy over my life? To this very day I still can see her face in my mind talking to me. We must have talked for about 45 minutes right there in the store, and when she left me she said, "Remember me, and when I see you in heaven, I'll be talking to you Pastor." I felt like this woman was trying to pull something out of me that I didn't know was there. Was she a messenger for God, telling me to step up my spiritual game? Was God telling me I need to help more people and do more for his kingdom, his glory? Have you ever had a complete stranger come up to you and just start talking to you about, your own future? If you ever have, take notice of what they are trying to say. If it's something useful and something you have already had on your heart and mind, you might want to dive a little deeper and give it some meditation or some overnight thought. However if it's completely useless to your life pattern thought process or goals throw it away quickly and don't give it room to grow. I remember an old Boss I had say to me, "When people say things to you and they don't feel right, don't give it room to grow in your head, you don't have any more room to rent in there." How fitting, people will come to you all day long with their problems and worries. You have enough of your own things to deal with, let alone their drama. This hinders your inner greatness, that small voice that communicates with you every day, directing your steps. Praying daily for direction and development has helped me tremendously. Recall King Solomon, prayed for wisdom and everything was added to him. You need to pray for specific things, pray for help in areas of your life where you struggle. One of my main constant prayers is to become a better man, husband, father, and for God to lead me in the direction he wants me to go, to develop my inner greatness, my inner spiritual strength. I am telling you, you are great! This book, these words you are reading came to me in a dream one morning, I got on my computer and I could not stop writing. What was that? It was my inner greatness screaming out saying, "You have something to say that can help someone, maybe save a life, don't be a scardy-cat and keep it to yourself!" Now that is my truth and it's what I believe. You can do the same thing and much more. Never forget that people will test your inner greatness. They will underestimate you and doubt your abilities, sometimes your own family members will do this to you. Remember that your dreams and your visions are your own, no one else's. There will be roadblocks along the way and people that will test your patience. Have you ever come up with an idea or had a plan to do something and then as soon as you shared that with someone they said, "You're crazy you'll never be able to do that." Now don't you believe those lies, people think that if they are not able to do something, then you will never be able to do it. I've seen too many people give up on their dreams simply because someone told them they could not achieve them. So they give up they don't go to the job interview, they don't go to practice, they don't finish college or even finish high school. It's easy to settle for less than your best it's easy to give up hope. Once you start to listen to your inner greatness you will begin to realize what it is that you need to be doing. Next you have to be in tune with your feelings, you have to be honest with yourself. When we are children we lie, cheat, steal but the question is, who taught us to do that? Often times we teach ourselves because the world that we live in is very corrupt full of political liars, church liars, every day liars. People then start to believe that being a liar is normal, because it has happened so much but the truth is it is very dark, we all know who the father of the first lie is no need to mention his name. People often misinterpret power with greatness. There are many great people with no power think on the local level, the grandmother that is the head of her household, the pastor that reaches people in his community and affects many lives, but then there is also the opposite. There are people who go on power trips and this power may come from their physical or financial strength or military power. Never forget that almost all power is abused. That is how we learn, we have to become strong inwardly and outwardly and some lust for power. Are any of these things you today? You cannot hide from the truth so you have to let go and humble yourself, look at the truth and fix the broken pieces. We all have our mistakes, our transgressions, our regrets. The first step though is to admit our errors and tell the universe that, Yes I may have done these things in the past but I know that I am a good person and I know that there is a divine direction for my life. Forgive me for my past mistakes and help me direct my steps forward in a new direction, a positive light. Atonement is the act of making good. So you go back and you talk to that person that you did wrong and you make it right. Take ownership, take responsibility of the people you cheated and the people you lied to and ask them for forgiveness. You will be surprised at what they have to say. In the end if you come to them with a humble heart and be sincere, that light will shine out through you and upon them forgiveness will be yours. You can act with love and kindness and that same love and kindness will be given back to you. Do you know how hard it is to stay mad at someone who is extremely nice to you? I know I can't do it. How can you stay mad at someone that comes to you humbly and ask you for forgiveness and promises not to do it again but is also smiling and willing to do anything to make it right. For as much as you forgive, you will be forgiven much and let's face it we all need forgiveness from the things that we have done in the past. Those things have helped develop you into the person that you are today. If you have not struggled you would not know what success truly feels like and this is the ultimate balance of life. We must struggle in order to understand what success feels like. You can have all the money in the world, all the riches, you can buy the best experiences life has to offer but a life without love honor and integrity is completely worthless. If you exercise power use it humbly, be benevolent, help others, live with passion and honor. You must look inside of yourself, what's inside will come out eventually. You've heard the saying, "what's done in the dark will eventually come to light." See your greatness as a place that is inside of you in the dark, yelling to come out and reveal itself to the world! Don't discount those feelings you have deep down inside, they were put there for a reason now it's up to you to find out why.

CHAPTER

Find Your Why

A YOUNG MAN WAS sitting at a bus stop when another man about the same age as him pulled up in front of him in a bright red Lamborghini the young man at the bus stop said to the man in the Lamborghini, how did you get that car, how did you become so successful? The man in the Lamborghini said if you really want to know, meet me tomorrow morning at 4 AM at the beach. The young man at the bus stop agreed and at 4 am the next morning he was at the beach. It was dark and cold there, so the successful man told the young man now if you want to understand how I achieve my success start walking into the water. The young man thought this is an odd request but proceeded to walk into the water. When the water got up to his knees he stopped and the successful man said keep going. The young man proceeded to walk in further and now the water was up to his waist and the successful man said keep going. The young man kept walking, now the water was up to his nose and he could hardly breathe and he wondered how far more he would have to go. The young man was in over his head he could barely swim and the successful man jumped into the water and saved his life and took him out of the water. The young man thought this guy is crazy, he doesn't want me to be successful he wants me to die. When they made it back to dry land the successful man asked the young man how did he feel walking out in the water in the darkness? The young man said, I was scared, I was wet I was cold, I didn't know what was going to happen next. The successful man said good, that is exactly how I got my success. I was walking into a territory that I did not know or understand I was scared and I was confused but I took a risk and I kept walking. The successful man said, as the water was starting to get into your nose what is the one thing that you wanted more than anything else? The young man said, I wanted to breathe. The successful man said exactly, when you want to be successful as much as you want to breathe then you will be successful. There will be times when we are unsure of our circumstances, we are unsure of our surroundings, it is dark and it is cold, we are all alone this is when you must develop your inner strength and tenacity and your faith must be rock solid. When you got up this morning Why did you do it? Is it because you had to go to work or school? What is your why? For many people it's their families, the commitments that they made. I say this respectfully, that's not good enough, and you have to do better than that. When Kobe Bryant won his first NBA championship everyone around him was celebrating everyone was extremely happy and proud for him, that's when Phil Jackson pulled him to the side and whispered in his ear, "You have to do better". That very summer Kobe Bryant was in the gym every single day in the early mornings working out all through the summer preparing for the next season with his coaches word constantly in his mind playing over and over again, "you have to do better." The next season Kobe Bryant not only won the championship again but became the most valuable player. What he did not know is that his coach used the same tactic on another player of his by the name of Michael Jordan. Six time NBA world champion Michael Jordan was told, you need to do better and the end result, he became the greatest of all time. You need that extra push, no matter how good you are, no matter how many things you have accomplished, you need to do better. This can apply in all aspects of life we all can do better, we can be better fathers, better mothers, we can be better students, we can be better friends. Think about what you can be better at today, maybe you need to a better boyfriend or a better girlfriend a better listener. Every day we are constantly learning constantly adapting to our environment to the things around us, it's up to us to make the world a better place to be better we must do better constantly. When Kobe Bryant was told that he needed to do better he didn't get angry he had the right perspective instead of talking back, instead of having a negative attitude that summer he put in so much work that he became better, you can be better you can do the same. We should never think so much of ourselves that we think we no longer have anything more to learn or do. We can learn a powerful lesson from Kobe Bryant, that even if we are at the top of our game we can always do more, we can always do better. Don't get offended if someone asked you to do better or do more than what is asked of you like a coworker or a boss they might just be testing you. I'll never forget when I started working one of my very first jobs I had a boss who is a real stickler for being on time he was a military man so what else could you expect. If you started work at 9 o'clock he expected you to be there at 9 o'clock or earlier. If you were a minute late you were called into his office and you were in big trouble. While everyone hated this supervisor I learned to appreciate him, it made me realize that being on time to events are important. He tested me, he stretched me to be better with my punctuality and professionalism, now I expect the same from my staff. People come into your life just like the seasons they're there for a little while and then they're gone but while they're there you have to appreciate what it is that they are trying to teach you and learn as much as you can from them. Have you figured out your why? Have you figured out why you do what you do and how you're going to get there? Finding your why means finding your purpose the reason for you. Do you believe in yourself? Do you have faith that you can do anything? You can do anything you set your mind, and heart upon so attend that conference, schedule that meeting, go back to school do whatever it takes to get where you want to be if the great one Kobe Bryant did, you can too! You have to do better!

CHAPTER

No Pain No Gain

ACTOR, AND PRO WRESTLER Dwayne "The Rock" Johnson, is one of the most disciplined people I know. He truly understands the principles of No Pain, No Gain. Here is an extremely successful man, who still works as if he has nothing. He gets up at very early hours of the morning to work out in the gym, then it's off to shoot, his TV shows and movies, jet setting all over the world. If you never heard his story he started as an amateur wrestler, getting paid only a few dollars, but he was doing what he loved to do. I had the privilege of not only meeting him, but running with him at the Revlon Run event for Cancer at the Coliseum in Los Angeles. He is a very nice man, with a big heart, for people and helping others. I wish more celebrities were like him. I've learned from him, when you work hard as if you have nothing, you will always have something. Everyone says they want to be successful, but what are they willing to sacrifice to have it? You have to be willing to lose sleep, you have to be willing to miss meals, you have to be willing to sacrifice your time away from your family. If one of your goals is to lose weight you have to be willing to sacrifice your time to be able to get up to go to the gym and to eat the right foods. You also have to be willing to invest in yourself, you have to be willing to be lonely to not have friends for a while unless your friends understand your goals and support you. There's no better feeling you get after you accomplish something that you were working very hard for no matter if it's losing weight or starting a savings account. Create small wins for yourself every single day and every day you'll inch closer to your goals. While you're making these sacrifices it's also important to not be greedy. What is greed? Some people like to say greed is good, but in reality greed is not good! By definition greed is gathering more then you actually need to the detriment of others. Greed is like a person who goes to rob a bank and steals $1 million dollars then goes back to the same bank five minutes later and tries to steal another $1 million dollars. I know that was a bad illustration, but I was trying to give you an idea of how that makes no sense at all. It's easy in this society to become a greedy person when we look at television and we see celebrities like Kim Kardashian, Beyoncé, Kanye West, Taylor Swift and many others buy multimillion dollar homes and drive expensive vehicles and live very luxurious lives it's easy for us to want that light and those same things. Why? It's Light! The reason why people are so fascinated by celebrities is because the light is always on them meaning the limelight everywhere they go. The media covers them and the light is always on them just like a spotlight if you can imagine, they are always visible they are always seen so people begin to think that they are more stable than they are. You begin to think and see the things that they have all the time the financial status that they possess the places that they travel to so you become drawn to them like you know them, like they're your friend, so you follow them on Instagram, Snapchat, Facebook which only increases their visibility increases their wealth and increases their fame. Being famous means that a lot of people know who you are it has nothing to do with wealth. Being famous does not mean you're wealthy. You could be famous for all the wrong things and still not have a dollar. The reason that celebrities become so attractive is because they put themselves in the light and they make themselves appear like they have it all together, like they are very stable individuals when often times they are very insecure, very scared people who live life in a box surrounded by bodyguards afraid of people that wish to hurt them. Having a lot of attention or having a lot of fanatical people that love what you do can be very dangerous. When Michael Jackson was alive he wasn't a normal person, he was a legend, he was a superstar. Michael Jackson would often talk about how he could not simply go to the mall, or walk down the street without being noticed and that notice would draw him so much attention that his fans would run to wherever he was and fanatical people can love you to death. I recall when I was working as a production assistant for the Jackson family for a TV show that they had running briefly but it was to be a show about the five brothers and what they're doing now. I will never forget my first day on set I was walking up to the studio and I saw a man smoking by a trailer and we started having a conversation and I remember the man telling me, "They have been dancing to our music for years and they will forever." He would then talk about recording and working in his new studio and how he was excited about the television show. After talking to him for about five minutes someone yelled out, "Tito let's go it's time to start recording the show." At that moment I realized I had been having a full on conversation with Tito Jackson and I had no clue. About 10 minutes later I went inside the studio and I started working with Jermaine Jackson, Tito Jackson, Marlon Jackson, Randy Jackson. Michael was nowhere to be found, and I actually did ask if he would be a part of the television show and I was told that he respectfully said no, he did not wish to be a part of it. I always thought to myself why did Michael make that decision? After pondering this question for about a month I think I figured it out. I realized that Michael Jackson, is a brand and he is bigger than a TV show and he separated himself from his brothers many years ago. He truly was the superstar of that family and anything that he was a part of had to be perfect. Michael Jackson made a sacrifice, he knew that he could not be the same as everyone else in his family, he sold millions of records on his own from his own albums. Focused on his own projects focused on his acting career and being in movies even though they were few and far between. He dedicated and he sacrificed everything for his career, even his health. I will never forget the day that he ended up in the hospital and eventually died. I was walking through a mall when I received a phone call from the show TMZ, how they got my cell phone number I will never know but they asked me if I knew anything about the current condition of Michael Jackson. I was in shock and I said, "What condition"? They said you haven't heard he's in the hospital right now something has happened to him can you please call the family for us and find out any information? I thought to myself sure I'll call the family but I won't give you any information out of respect for the family and out of respect for Michael. TMZ was trying to be the very first media outlet to break the story of what was happening to Michael Jackson at that moment but I was a huge fan of Michael Jackson and I'd listened to his music all my life so whatever I learned I would not share. Sometime later that day the family confirmed that he died. It was the saddest day musically for me. This was someone I looked up to professionally, he was an extremely smart businessman so much more than an artist the King of Pop may he rest in peace. What I learned more than anything from the example of his life and death was that Michael wasn't afraid to make a sacrifice to be what he wanted to be. He wasn't afraid to be different, he wasn't afraid to stand alone and do business alone even if other people didn't like it or understand it. Translate that into your life, don't be afraid to walk alone, don't be afraid to like it. Don't be afraid to take risks and be in uncomfortable situations. You've heard the words comfort zone, you must do what it takes to get out of that area in your life and in your finances, stop living so comfortable always doing the same thing you're used to. Take action! Surround yourself with people who are movers and shakers, people who believe the same as you do and are trying to better themselves. People that understand true sacrifice people that are in the same field that you would like to be in, the people that are currently doing what you want to do become friends with them remember being friends with people like this is as good as cash in the bank. Ask yourself what am I willing to sacrifice? Is it my time, my money or energy? When you're ready to make this step just as the successful man said to the younger man, you will be ready. Nowadays people are all talk, they are very quick to brag, very quick to say what they can do but yet do nothing at all, stay away from those influences. You see it every day on social media on Facebook, Instagram, Snapchat people posting what they have and yet most of them don't have that at all it's all perception/false appearances. Don't let yourself fall into that trap, the trap of keeping up with the Joneses and I know many people like that if you have one dollar in your pocket they will be quick to show you that they have two dollars in theirs. I know one guy who is so quick to brag about his lifestyle and the money that he makes and the job that he has that he doesn't even realize he's a braggart. What he fails to realize is that he is a single guy with no real responsibilities, no children, no wife, just him. Any person without family knows it's very easy when you only work for yourself and 100% of the money that you make goes in your pocket, but when you become a man and you have a family and you have responsibilities and you have to pay actual bills the money that you make is no longer yours you must sacrifice what you have for others and this is what this braggart fails to realize. He will never realize it until he has a real responsibilities and real things to pay for, living the single life is easy but once you take on these new responsibilities, these family responsibilities your lifestyle changes you start to understand real sacrifices. You will sacrifice a meal to ensure that your wife and children eat, you will sacrifice your time with them to go to work to provide for them, you will sacrifice everything that you have just to make sure they have a roof over their head clothes on their back a vehicle to drive and food on the table. I never really understood what sacrifice was until I became a father. That single act changed my whole perspective, it wasn't getting married and having a wife, it was actually when my first daughter was born and I held her in my arms for the first time and I realized this little person will depend on me for the rest of her life or at least until she becomes an adult but even then she will still need her father's loving advice and arms to carry her through life. I still reach out to my mom and dad to this day, for life advice and to ask them questions on what they think about certain topics I appreciate my mom and dad so much for they have sacrificed so much for me to raise myself and my two older brothers. I saw their struggle when I was younger and it's not until you get older and have children of your own that you really understand the true sacrifice that they made to feed, clothe and house you so if you never said thank you to your parents or the person that raised you, could've been a grandmother or anyone tell them thank you because it's not easy to raise children. They made a sacrifice to be with you to raise you to provide for you. Maybe it was a teacher or mentor that you had that went out of their way to stay with you longer after school to show you something or teach you something that you never knew that was a sacrifice on their part never forget those people that molded you into the person that you are today. Go back to that school and thank them, shake their hand take them out for a cup of coffee or meal show them that you appreciate what they did for you I promise you it will mean more to them than you could ever imagine. Having a heart of gratitude, a spirit of appreciation is extremely important it shows the universe that you appreciate everything that comes your way and you will be blessed with even more when you show appreciation to others. Look around, look at your family, coworkers, peers and loved ones it's time to reach out to them and say thank you for their sacrifice, their ultimate sacrifice.

CHAPTER

Microwave Society

WE LIVE IN A very now society where everything is instant, everything is like a microwave. The fact is most people want things so fast that they don't even want to put in the work to achieve success. People want things that are already prebuilt, premade, preset why do you think some women are attracted to married men? Because those women don't want to put in any work to find a man, they'd much rather have a man that is already built, already in a relationship, a prebuilt man, a man that is stable, a man that is working, a man with a job, a man who already has a family and isn't really looking to build another family with her. That's what I like to call a man who is already been microwaved. A man who is already ready. Nowadays people don't want to put in the work.

They don't want to look for a job they want to job handed to them. They want to be hooked up so they don't have to look for anything at all. You cannot be this type of person if you wish to achieve any kind of life goal or success you would have to be the working person, the creative person, the builder. You can become a builder and you must be a builder even if you have never developed this trait before, now is the time to start. You have to be a people builder you have to be able to encourage others. If you have children you need to build that child into the person that you want them to be. Your words are very powerful when you speak to your children and other family members, you can either build them up or tear them down, you possess this power. You must speak life over your children. People in general are very unstable very unsure of themselves they need all the positive words that you can muster, they need to hear that you're proud of them, that you love them, that you support them, that if they need any type of help whatsoever that you will be there for them always. People are very insecure they need that added confidence boost every single day they may not say it but trust me, they need it, they need to hear daily encouragement from you. Tell them how smart they are, how talented they are, how beautiful they are. The more positive things you tell them on a daily basis it will sink down into their spirit person into their mind in their subconscious and they will never forget it so when that negativity comes to them in the world at school or wherever they may be they have been built up and been created to be such strong individuals that you have already counteracted all the negativity that the people will try to throw their way. They will remember how smart they are talented and beautiful how you planted those seeds in them every day in their young life that now that they're older they will not settle for less they will not settle for negativity they will not settle for individuals who are not positive like they are it will act like an invisible shield that they will carry with them throughout their life and it's all because of you. You built them up you lifted their spirits up you helped them grow into the person that they are now it is because of you that they are positive that there light will shine not only on themselves but every person that they are around. Did you know that you are actually a flashlight? I want you to see yourself as a flashlight. Have you ever wondered why you were put at your current job? Have you ever wondered why you attend the church that you do? Have you ever wondered why you attend the school that you attend now? You are a flashlight, let me explain. If you walk into a dark place without a flashlight, what do you see? You see darkness, you probably wouldn't even be able to see one foot in front of you or your hands if you were to place them in front of your very face. However if you have a flashlight you can turn it on and you'll be able to see everything that is around you very clearly. Imagine that the place where you work, the place where you go to school, and the place where you go to church is a very dark place. Then you walk in remember you're a flashlight, The moment you walk in, you light up the room you're a flashlight and the purpose of you, is to shine light on every room every person every interaction that you have throughout the day. Your job is to shine a positive light everywhere you go you are a flashlight. So if you're wondering why you have that job, why you go to that church, why you attend that school it's because someone their needs your light, needs your help and you need to be the light. You need to be the flashlight that someone needs in their life right now. I guarantee there is someone that you talk to pretty much on a daily basis who always brings you there troubles their worries their concerns their stress and you say a couple words to them and you brighten their day just like the flashlight that I know you are. You're not only a flashlight you're a people builder and we can always use more people builders in the world there's enough negativity out there already enough famine, enough wars, enough trouble. I would love to be able to turn on the news in the morning and hear nothing but positive stories but what I've learned is that the news doesn't report on positive stories, for the most part they report on what gets them ratings, which is negative reports, who killed who, who got robbed, who got kidnapped here's another high-speed chase, this is what gets people to watch them it's bad news not good news and watching too much news can make you very depressed so I have limited my News watching, why do I want to hear the same story day in and day out over and over again. The only thing I listen too now on the news will probably be the weather report and that's wrong half the time so why should I add any more stress or hear any more bad news. Yes it is good to know what's going on in general but watching the news all day just makes you depressed there's nothing positive about it. They may do one or two feel-good stories but those are far and few in between. I've noticed that in other countries there news is a lot different than the news in America. Other countries actually do show some positive news stories a bit more than what you see here and there news broadcasts are much different and if you've ever seen any you know exactly what I mean. Not everyone can be a people builder, a motivator yes there are people who would like nothing more than to see you fail and not reach your goals for whatever reason they may think that you're out to take their job or take their spouse or whatever it may be and they may view you as a threat and that's OK because let me tell you not everyone is going to like you, not everyone is going to be for you not everyone will have your best interest at heart some may call them haters. The haters will judge you and really want nothing to do with you they will talk behind your back because small minds have nothing better to do than talk about people, they will smile in your face and talk about you behind your back guaranteed. And once you become successful and you start running your own business and you start doing your own thing they will talk about you even more they are jealous of you and you don't need to associate with them at all. Keep going forward and being your best every day, they will hate you even more and that's fine remember your goals and remember your purpose you're not doing it for them you're doing it for you. You will lose friends, you will gain friends you will learn people's true intentions and why they are around you. A few years ago a friend of mine won the lottery he won $56 million dollars. He even tried to be anonymous but the word still got out, his family and friends found out that he won the lottery and that's when the phone calls started to pour in. I saw my poor friend get phone calls from everyone under the sun people he hadn't spoken to in years started blowing up his cell phone and the pastor was calling, his cousins were calling, his coworkers were calling even his boss was calling. People that he hadn't spoken to in 20 years magically remembered his phone number and decided to give him a call almost the next day after he won the $56 million dollars. I thought that was so fascinating how could they all of a sudden remember who he was now that he was rich. Now all of a sudden everyone needed something, everyone had a need to tell him congratulations. It's interesting how they never called him before how they never needed him before how they never cared about his family before. It's very sad to think this way but this is how people are they will see your success and want their success to be microwaved to be given a handout. The question is if they won $56 million dollars would they reach out to you? Probably not. So now everyone is calling him, his phone is ringing nonstop to the point where he has to change his phone number but not only change his phone number change his address. My friend ended up moving to Texas he packed up all his belongings his wife and kids and they end up buying a beautiful ranch style home in Texas filled with horses and cattle he basically bought a farm and that's where they live now. He did make a few donations to close family members and friends and invested the rest very wisely. He was a Filipino man from humble beginnings but he always knew that he would win the lottery one day and he even told me several times that he would win he was so sure of himself that he predicted his own future. He did what I'm asking you to do he proclaimed his future he told the universe what he wanted and the universe listened and got out of his way and granted him a super large gift. He would often talk about how his lottery win would be soon on the way he never doubted himself but he walked around claiming his victory even before he had it, he knew it was coming he just did not know when. What are you claiming over your life? Are you claiming victory? Are you claiming success? If you're not, you need to start right away. Never say things like I'm not going to win anyway, it doesn't make a difference, I'm not going to even try. Those negative words can push you back to a place where you may not return from. Why don't you turn it around speak about your successes before it even happens, you must claim it, you must own it, it must be yours and you can do this just like my friend did. Have you had your eye on something for a long time? Is it a new car, a new house, a new job, a child? Claim it before it comes! I knew a woman who wanted to have a baby she wanted it so bad her husband and herself would try and had been trying for years to conceive a child but no success. They would go to doctors and see specialists and pay tons of money to try to ensure they would have a baby they did everything in their power to make it happen but it wouldn't. Finally the couple decided they would stop seeing the specialist and just wait and start to claim it so the wife decided to decorate a special room for the baby. She bought a crib and diapers along with baby clothes at the time. She was doing this and she was not pregnant but she thought to herself if I want to have a baby I need to claim it and I need to act as if the baby is already on the way and that's what she did, she fully decorated that room for a brand new bundle of joy. About a month later the room stayed intact and she went for a physical and the doctor said you're about one month pregnant. What happened? The moment she started to act on what she wanted and truly claim it was the moment she became pregnant she became pregnant with her dream she was finally about to have a baby. She took action even before she knew it was about to come true, are you taking action? You must act in accordance with your dreams because the things you want are already there but you must act upon them if you wish to receive them take action, you can, you will. Are you pregnant today? No I don't mean pregnant meaning you have a baby inside of you, but are you pregnant with dreams? Hopes? The answer to that question is yes you are very pregnant with dreams, hopes, aspirations in your heart mind and soul. It's time for you to give birth, it's time for you to give birth to those dreams hopes and aspirations. When my wife was pregnant and it was getting close for her to give birth she was very uncomfortable, very stressful it's the same way with our hopes and dreams. When it's time for our dreams to be born it's a very stressful uncomfortable time in our lives but once we do give birth to the dream it is a beautiful experience and it is everything that we have hoped for just like that child that was born. Birds build there nests from broken branches. Maybe today you have broken dreams, that have taken a very long time to put together, but once it all comes together, you will feel an amazing accomplished feeling! Put the pieces together, it will not be microwaved, but it will happen sooner than you think, when you take action, claim it, and believe you can. We are so used to this fast food lifestyle, where everything is drive-through or Microwaved to the point where society has ripped away our patience or ability to be able to wait for anything. We are not taught patience, we learn patience. I personally cannot stand to be late to anything I even hate being late to the movies, I actually enjoy seeing the previews, I enjoy seeing what's about to come out. I had to learn patience dealing with my wife. If you have a wife, girlfriend or mother then you understand how long it takes for a woman to get ready for any event. When they say they are ready you already know that is an additional 40 minute wait time, like I said I had to learn patience. Women are Gods wonderful beautiful creatures so you have to be patient with them you have to be understanding with them. You cannot understand all of their needs wants or desires but the best thing you can do is be honest, open and kind, but most of all be a listener more than a talker, develop patience. The microwave has one job and that is to heat things up very quickly try not to live in this manner, try not to be angry. Nothing good happens when we're angry we can't think straight and we can't make rational decisions. Never make decisions when you're upset develop levelheadedness stay calm cool and collected. Often times when we are angry we make all the wrong decisions, decisions that we regret later on in life. You cannot expect to move forward from a place of anger, You cannot expect to be your best if you are angry so take some time out of your day to really think about what it is that is bothering you and analyze it and think of it from a place of peace. Realize that no matter how bad you think it is there is always a solution and if you come at it from a place of peace you will find all of your answers. Did you know that no one can make you angry but yourself? Don't give anyone else that power or control the power to control your emotions. You are in control of your happiness and you are in control of your anger, which one will you choose? You can choose to be happy or you can choose to be angry and bitter. The choice is yours, and just like the microwave these emotions can come within a few seconds. Choose wisely.

CHAPTER

Change Your Perspective

THERE WAS AN OLD man, who decided he wanted to move into a retirement home. He went to the receptionists desk, and she proceeded to show him to his potential home lodgings. As they were walking up the stairs, she started telling the man about the features of the room, she said it has very big windows, the old man said, "I love it"! She said it has central air, the old man said, "I love it, I'll take it." She said wait until you see the size of the bed and the TV in the room. The old man said, I love it, I'll take it! She said, "hold on you haven't even seen the room." He said, "It doesn't matter, I am already expecting goodness, and that is what I'll find." The old man saw the room, and fell even more in love. What did he do? He set his mind on goodness and had a heart of expectancy, and it followed him. Do you do that? Or do you worry about every little thing? There once was a man that was taking his friend to the hospital to have surgery, he dropped off his friend at the front and went to park his car. As he got out of his car and was walking to the hospital entrance a car hit him, and now both men were having surgery in the hospital at the same time. While they were doing the surgery they found a severe form of cancer in the man that got hit by the car. The doctors told him that they needed to remove the cancer right away otherwise it could be life ending for him very soon. The doctors were able to remove the cancer and save the man's life. On the surface getting hit by a car is a terrible life changing incident, but if he had not been hit in the first place, he never would have discovered the sickness in his body and have it removed. The man was very grateful that he got hit by the car, because it ultimately saved his life. His perspective was instantly changed from upset he got hit, to Thank God, he got hit. The Doctor who did his surgery was an extremely busy man, performing several procedures daily, seeing many patients. One day he was doing a physical on one of his older patients a woman was 85 years old and she could tell that something was not right with the doctor. The doctor told the woman that physically she looked ok and that she should make an appointment to see him again in the next 6 to 8 months for another routine physical. The woman then asked the doctor, how are you doing, you look stressed. The doctor thought this was an odd question, no one ever normally ask how the doctor is doing but it's the other way around. The doctor went on to admit to the old woman that he lives a very busy lifestyle. He told her that he spends 80 hours a week at work and hardly has time to see his wife or children and that when he does see his wife and children he so angry because he's always at work. The old woman told the doctor how she is all alone how her husband died years ago and her children all moved out of state along with her grandchildren. She said how she would long to hear the pitter patter of little feet in her house again how she would long to hear laughter or have someone to talk to at night how she is very lonely. The old woman wished she could be young again and wished that she could have the life that the doctor took for granted. This changed the doctor's perspective, he went home that night and gave his children the biggest hug, his children were very young about three and five years old and gave a big kiss to his wife. That one conversation with the old woman changed the doctor's perspective. He viewed his life and his living situation with new eyes, with eyes of appreciation and love. Do you sometimes do that? It's easy for us to get caught up in work caught up with the day-to-day activities that we miss out on our loved ones activities, going to their school plays or soccer games or arts and crafts events. It's time you put things in the right perspective, remember we talked about having discipline and having order. It's so easy to see the same people every day and start to take them for granted you neglect the things that they do for you every day. There was a very rich man who decided he would teach his son a lesson about how poor people lived so that his son would appreciate all that the rich father had done for him. The rich father decided to take his son to visit a poor family to spend the night, the father and son together. The rich father and son stayed with the poor family that night. The next day as they were driving back home the rich father asked his son, Son what did you learn about staying with the poor family? He said, I learned that they have four dogs we only have one, I learned that we have many lights attached to our house but they have all the stars in the sky. I learned that we have a big pool in the backyard but they have an entire river. I learned that they laugh and talk at the dinner table together all night while we are stuck on our electronic devices in our rooms. I want to say, thank you Dad for taking me on this trip overnight to show us how poor we really are. The rich father's plan had backfired! His son had a completely different perspective than he had. We are not born with the concept of rich or poor we learn the concept of rich or poor, we are born with nothing and when we die we return back to that nothing. Our society always paints the picture that with more money you will have more happiness, however there are many miserable wealthy people, and miserable poor people. Money does not equal happiness, you determine your own happiness. Develop the right perspective and you will see happiness everywhere you go. You will find joy in everything you do. How do you see yourself? Are you happy or angry? The universe will not respond to your anger or frustration it will not give you what you need if you are like that. Years ago I had a coworker who was very negative, she had worked for the same company for many years with no promotions.

She was known as the trouble maker in the office, she was always looking to get someone in trouble, while always trying to make herself look good. I bet you work with someone or know someone like that right now! She was a real fire starter and she often wondered why upper management treated her so bad all the time. It's because upper management could see right through her, through her games and negative attitude, and they wanted nothing to do with her. She was always talking about how much more work she did as compared to her peers, always talking when the boss was trying to talk. I say this respectfully, you have to learn to shut your mouth! No one likes someone who is always talking nonsense. This woman never figured out that all she had to do, was shut her mouth, keep her head down and work! She had seen many examples of people who got hired after her and in a few months get promoted above her. Why was that? They were doing something she was not. They tuned out the negativity, stopped talking, and stayed focused on themselves. They weren't worried about making the boss look bad, or creating friendships at work, they just worked hard and promoted themselves. Once your willing to change your perspective that's when the boss and everyone else will look at you differently. Be a constant professional in your work place, show up early, cut out unnecessary chit chat, and focus more on your work than your cell phone. One of the things bosses hate the most is seeing someone watching TV or playing games while they are on the clock, it makes you look unproductive and unprofessional. How does your boss view you? How do you view yourself? What changes do you need to make in order to get promoted? What are you going to do differently? I'll never forget the boy who's dream it was to play professional baseball for the Detroit Tigers but he hurt his leg in his early 20's and never got the opportunity. His Dad never believed in him that he would ever be good enough and when he got hurt, that was his Dad's confirmation. His Dad told his son to go look for a job and the son had a friend who owned a restaurant. The son asked his friend for a job and told him you don't even have to pay me I just have to be out of the house so my dad will think I have a job. He got a job making pizzas in the back of the kitchen. Soon after that he became very good at making pizzas and developed his own recipes and started his own restaurant. He was humble enough to start at the bottom and work for free in order to gain experience that he needed. Today we all have eaten a slice from Little Caesar's pizza. Not only that, he became so successful that he ended up buying The Detroit Tigers baseball team. God had a plan for him even back then, he went from wanting to play baseball to owning the baseball team, what a huge blessing! We don't know the end plans that God has for us. The only thing we can do is keep moving forward every day and be our best each moment. However when we humble ourselves as this man did we put ourselves in position, in alignment for great things. We should not think more of ourselves or boast or brag about certain opportunities but rather be thankful for them be thankful for the job, thankful for everything. My father was a bus driver, for many years. My father did what he loved to do, drive. He loved being a driver, he loved driving long distances he had a passion for it, and got paid to do it. Some days were good, some not so good, but he had the right perspective he kept doing his best and being on time, until he retired. My mom was the same way, she was a cafeteria manager for the public school system doing her best everyday, making sure the children had enough to eat, as well as cooking meals for myself and my two brothers every night. These two are my heroes. They have been married for forty plus years, and if I can have half of their success I will feel like I have made it in my life. They are the example and backbone of our family. Their relationship is far from perfect, a lot of forgiveness and understanding was needed to make it this far, but I am proud of the family they raised and I am proud of them. They taught us perspective, never take things for granted and have a follow through mentality, never give up, on your relationships or goals.

CHAPTER

9

Your Trouble Is Your Blessing

WHERE WOULD YOU BE without the mistakes you made in the lessons you learned from them? We all have done things in our past that we are not proud of. The good news is you're not defined by your past or held back by your mistakes. You actually are prepared by your past think about all the things that you have gone through that have developed your character develops your inner strength. If it had not been for the struggle or the lack you would not appreciate the blessings or the successes that you have recently. I talk to many parents who have a few kids and I always like to ask them, did you plan to have your children? I would say a good 95% of the answers are No, we did not plan to have children they just happened. Children are a gift from God. I can honestly say for my three children we did not plan them, they were a gift. They were a gift in my immaturity that I was not ready to receive. I was not ready to be a father even though I had many strong male influences in my life, I am not afraid to say that it scared me deeply. I wanted to make sure that I would be able to take care of them and provide for them. I grew up seeing many kids without a dad and I could start to see the effect that growing up like that had on them. There was a blessing in my fear, but there was trouble in my heart. A few months back my neighbor accidentally hit my car from the front causing damage to the front and all of the electronics of the car. It was an older model BMW but I really liked that car and I thought that I would be able to keep it much longer. I took it to mechanic after mechanic and they weren't able to fix it quite the way that it was before. After some time I decided to get another car and I was able to get a truck, a much newer car, that trouble was my blessing. We are all being prepared for something greater. You may be in trouble today and you may not understand it, but trust and believe something is being developed in you right now. If it had not been for this, you would not be prepared for that. Lack and struggle are temporary, just like pain. Trouble is inevitable, but misery is optional. When you're faced with an unexpected challenge it's easy to get down on yourself and think I'm not going to give my best, I will not have faith, I will not even try. If it were easy to be successful everyone would be successful. There is always a lesson in the loss there is always a lesson that comes with the trouble. Have you seen that before in your life? You're doing good, moving along in life and then, BAM! An accident, a financial setback, a loved one dies, and just like that, your perfect world starts to fall apart in an instant. Good times and bad fall on all of us, it's normal to fall down, but what's not normal is to stay down. I know people that have been divorced for twenty years and still want to talk about what he did wrong Or what she did wrong. It was twenty years ago, let it go, move on. The longer you harp on how he hurt you or how she did you wrong, you're wasting your time and ruining the next blessing that is coming your way. There is an old saying that goes, "If you complain you remain." I have seen this very principle play out in my own life. You keep complaining about your grouchy husband, he's going to stay that way. You keep complaining about the fact your wife can't cook the way you like, she going to keep doing it that way. You keep complaining about your job, you're going to be stuck in that position for another ten years. Stop complaining! It won't do you any good to complain all the time, it's negative and besides that, nobody wants to hear you. People respond much better to praise than anything else."You catch more flies with honey, than you do with vinegar" Choosing your words wisely and using sweeter words has an instant good affect on people. When you come in contact with people, when you first see them, smile and say good morning, even if they don't smile back, they will remember what you did and the next time they see you, they will smile back. Never be afraid to extend a complement. It's ok to build someone else up, start to notice the people around you. Don't be afraid to say, "You look nice today", or my favorite "Are you losing weight?" you would not believe how people's faces light up brighter than new lights on a Christmas tree, when you say that! People need constant encouragement. They may not admit it, but they do. People are extremely shy and insecure, if you're not congratulations, that means you're a people builder and you can help others today! When someone is in trouble you can be the help they need. Often times they will need a shoulder to cry on, a hug or just someone to listen to them while they talk for a while. You can make the difference in someone's life today, and possibly save a life. Everyone needs someone to talk too, a friend, mentor, co-worker, we all have that go to person, we like to talk to when things turn into trouble. Remember everything is about to turn around for you, for your good, it may take some time, the legal battle, the sickness, the stress, the child that is acting up in school, these troubles are all about to be resolved, you can trust, the divine plan has already been established for your life. You were created to win, to thrive! Don't worry about your mortgage, your bills, your children, your spouse. No! Let Go and Let God! Let him handle it all, Pray, "Father God I lift up all my troubles to you this day. I know that you have me in the palm of your mighty hand. You provide for the birds of the air, so I know that you will provide much more for me. I believe and declare that you are the only one in the universe that can provide all my needs by your riches and glory. I lay my burdens down and have faith in you, I know that you are the only one who can help me. I ask for your wisdom in making all of my decisions, in my life. Please heavenly father, direct my steps in the way you want me to go. I trust that your ways are better than mine, please forgive me for my sins and shortcomings, I repent of my sins come into my heart, I make you my lord and savior, Amen." When we finally, let go, it's such a freeing experience, we know that everything we do will be taken care of by our Father. Get in a good church and bible study speak with people about positive things, like God, and his plan for your life. I promise it will be better than the one you have for yourself. What's so amazing about God, is that he knew you would get yourself into trouble, even before you did the wrong doing. Yet he loves you so much he sent his son to die and take away your sins, your trouble. He turned your trouble into your blessing, your salvation! Why not have a new attitude? Recognize that God has your best interest at heart, and he is the great redeemer of that trouble you put yourself in, put your head up and put your shoulders back. Today you are forgiven for the trouble, today you are a new creation.

CHAPTER

10

Invoke, Don't Be Broke

I NEED YOU TO start speaking strong positive things about yourself, right now. Say "A great financial prize is about to fall into my lap" "Health and wealth are upon my life." As you invoke you create exactly what you need. Begin to state your needs so they can start to solidify. Prayer is a form of invocation, especially when we pray out loud, we have to pray with the heart of believing and knowing, without any doubts in our heart and mind. How can you ask for something, but you really don't believe you're going to get it? When the shamans of old called for rain and it suddenly rained down buckets, everyone thought it was some kind of great magical act. But people didn't understand how the process work. It was only the power of invocation with a bit of help from the shamans connections. When we speak out loud, when we verbalize our thoughts we engage the manifestation process. Sound is a part of that which creates a reality. Each moment of our life we either invoke or destroy our dream. We have to invoke our desires and call them out to the universe. Be firm. Be absolutely sure invoke your dreams as fact. By invoking your dreams as fact you bring it to the here and right now. Don't daydream don't voice any maybes or uncertainty or doubt. You have to be careful when you invoke because you will get exactly what you asked for and maybe what you ask for is it really what you wanted. Remember not to engage in idle chatter and thoughtless remarks if you say, "This situation is a nightmare then your invoking terrible spirits, if you say, "It's a dreadful you establish fear and dread in your life. Don't moan and don't allow doubt, if you're worried about something keep it to yourself and don't vocalize it is fact work instead on the solution and voice that solution as fact. Everything can be changed, never underestimate the power of your words if you don't like the world you have previously made with your words of lack and limitation you can begin building a new world of limitless good and prosperity by changing your words and thoughts. Thoughts and words become things. What kind of things do you want in your life success or lack? Sorrow or Joy? It's just like my friend that won the lottery that I spoke about in the previous chapters he called it before he saw it, he claimed it before he received it, he was invoking what he knew to be true. He didn't know when he just knew it was going to happen and you can do the same.

Never say, when my promotion comes, say my promotion is coming. Never say when I find a job, say my job is coming. Never say when I find a spouse, say my spouse is coming. Never say when I have a child, say my child is coming. Invoke, invoke and you won't be broke. When you get paid it's easy to look at your check and think I have to pay this bill, that bill and then before you know it almost the same day that you got paid is the same day that you're broke again then what happens you immediately get depressed when you look at your bank account and you think I'll never get ahead, I'll never climb out of this debt, I will never overcome my financial burdens. Why don't you turn it around, why don't you think a different way why don't you be happy and think to yourself I am accomplished! I pay my bills and now I am blessed because I am working and I know that everything that I pay brings me closer to my goals. The bills cannot set you back, the bills can only set you up and show that you're a responsible human being. So pay that bill on time build up your credit score, so that you can one day buy what you really want, maybe a new house or car. Those setbacks are only a set up to propel you to your destiny, a better future for you and your family. No one likes paying bills but you have to do it. If you don't pay your phone bill what happens? They are very quick to turn it off. If you don't pay your cable bill, they are very quick to turn it off. The same with the light bill, the gas bill and everything else if you don't pay, they turn it off. Never worry about the minor things just put your head down and keep working. Every day is your opportunity to work and provide, pay bills, be creative use your mind come up with ideas. Forget the lack, forget the struggle, focus on success, abundance, growth, promotion think about the things you want and plant them deeply in your heart mind and soul and focus only on that. Don't let your mind wander on what if's and maybes, remember those do not belong in your vocabulary anymore. Your new words are yes, I can, I will. You have to turn around because right now is your opportunity! As you're reading along in this book I hope you're starting to understand the prevailing message, the message of creation, words and opportunity are yours to win. Napoleon Hill wrote the book Think and Grow Rich, I highly recommend this book. I also recommend the book the Fred Factor. In both of these wonderful books we learn the art of thinking and providing great customer service no matter what field of work we might be in both books cover things like planning, development, invoking and taking action towards accomplishing a dream. We learned that in order to be your best every day takes thought and planning. When Henry Ford the famous automaker decided he wanted to build cars that took a lot of thought, he had a lot of doubters, a lot of people did not share his vision a lot of people did not understand the dream that was in his heart and many did not support him at first, but he pressed forward and look at where Ford motor cars is today! Emmitt Smith, The Hall of Fame Dallas Cowboys running back was always told that he was too small to be a running back that he didn't quite fit the image of a pro football player. But he did not let that deter him he still went out every day and did his best and look where it landed him. He made himself a champion he made himself one of the greatest running backs of all time. What am I saying? They had an inner belief into greatness and they invoked what they knew to be true they had greatness inside of them just like you and I. They didn't let the naysayers or the complainers or the negative people stop them from what they knew was deep inside of them. You may be surrounded by them today but you don't have to listen to them. Just look around there are countless examples of people who are winning every single day. We all love underdog stories the stories that say against all odds this team with this person won it all. I don't know about you but I love a good comeback story. Look at the Rocky movies starring Sylvester Stallone. If you've never read his story of overcoming disability and homelessness please look it up! I love the way in those movies you see him going for a long jog around the city working on his goals working on his dreams so determined so full of passion and life. Then finally you see Rocky in the ring and he's fighting and he's punching but he's losing, he's getting hit in the stomach he's getting hit in the face and you think that there is no hope for him at all but then he turns it around and he starts getting stronger he starts fighting better and then eventually he wins, he wins the fight. We all have a little Rocky in us. Our fight is on a daily basis it's with our spouse, it's with our kids, it's with the traffic, it's with our boss, it's with our coworkers, but in the end you Win! I don't know about you but I love to win, I love to feel accomplished, I love to be able to reach a goal. This year the company that I work for set a goal to make $1 million dollars. It had never been done by a small group of people before in the history of the company to generate $1 million dollars through sales. We accepted the challenge and got to work, we didn't know how we would do it we just knew that we would and we started selling every single day and we eventually hit our $1 million dollar goal a month ahead of schedule by November 30 we had already reach the $1 million dollar mark. How did we do it? We believed that we could and we never doubted ourselves. We did something that had never been done in the company before and we told them that we were going to do it. As a team we invoked what we knew to be true even before it was we started an action plan a sales strategy, We planned out our days to the very dollar and we knew what we had to make every single day of the year in order to reach our goal yes, it was simple math but having that math figured out helped to keep us on target with our goals every day. We used a white board to help keep track of the numbers we used motivational quotes posted around our office that we would read throughout the day to help give us that extra push of motivation. We did whatever it took to keep us motivated we created daily incentives to keep the staff motivated gave out prizes and gift cards. Whatever we could do to keep everyone engaged we feel truly made the difference for our team. We didn't do anything super spectacular we just accomplished our goal you can do the same with your office or your students or your team put a goal in front of them and expect them to achieve it. We would give them a game plan and provide them the right incentives in order to want them to achieve it. Make it fun for them and you will be amazed by the results and you will have success and it will be a good time along the way.

CHAPTER

Madness

"To those who have, more shall be added." You've heard the expression, "The rich get richer and the poor get poorer." When I first started thinking about this, I didn't really understand it. You mean to tell me, if I have a lot, I will get more, but if I have little, I will stay with little? That is exactly what it means! We live in a world today that is extremely unbalanced financially. We have extreme levels of riches and extreme levels of poverty. The reality is our world will never be equal financially, there will be rich countries and poor countries and people all over the world will be both. I am an American citizen. I live in one of the most profitable but also in debt countries on the planet. How is it possible that we are rich and poor at the same time? Just look at New York, then visit Detroit.

It's economics, it's borrowing from other countries, all of these things come into play. We see our corporations become larger and richer while the people who work for these corporations don't see any kind of real increase financially, unless you're the CEO. The gap is widening and the middle class is shrinking to the point where there looks to be only rich or poor. This is why having a positive attitude goes along without saying. The more you moan and say you don't have enough the more it slips away from you. So constantly tell yourself that you're wealthy. Being wealthy is a way of viewing life. You're wealthy right now, you have good health, good friendships, a decent job then you already have more than most. I recall listening to Steve Harvey and I remember him saying that he had asked his father how he could help poor people and his father responded by saying, "don't be one of them". What his father was saying was that if you are poor yourself you can't help anyone, not even yourself. This is very true, you have to have some sort of resources if you are willing to help others. No matter if you are rich or homeless today you have something to be thankful for. Even if you are extremely poor you can be thankful that you are alive, you can be thankful that you can walk or see no matter what your financial situation is today you have something to be thankful for. Have you ever heard the expression to whom much is given, much is expected? We are the ambassadors, you are the ambassadors of the earth's vast resources. Don't be greedy, it's time to stop the madness! There is enough food on this planet, there is enough money on this planet for everyone. People are always saying that the world is overpopulated but there are many places on the planet where no one lives. There are an estimated eight or nine billion people on this planet and there are many things and life beings that yet have gone undiscovered, we have so much to learn about ourselves, our planet and our environment. We have many starving nations and while our country does provide aid to a lot of other countries, there are still plenty of places that need help. It starts with you! That orphanage, the foundation, that nonprofit, that cancer organization or AIDS organization that you have inside of your heart to begin, what's holding you back? The purpose of this book once again is to ask those deep questions, those things that you know you're supposed to do yet have not started. Make the call, license the product, set up the meeting, make the arrangements to move forward today. Time is slipping away from you at this very moment. Once you finish reading this chapter do something immediate, do something deliberate that will help you inch closer to your goal. Be a cheerleader for yourself. If no one believes in you and no one supports you, you support yourself! People that chase their dreams are not normal people, they are go-getters they are determined, they will not stop until they reach their goal. Famous Actor Will Smith once said in an interview that he has a treadmill mentality. He said if you challenge him to run on a treadmill to see who could run the longest amount of time, two things would happen. He said that either he would keep running on the treadmill to ensure that he would beat his competition or he would die. Do you understand the level of a competitor if he is willing to die? There is no way you can win against someone who is that dedicated, against someone who you know will never quit until you quit or he dies. This is the true meaning of dedication. You have to dedicate yourself to your dreams, goals and ideas and you have to have the mentality that you will either accomplish your dream or you will die. What impresses me the most about Will Smith is that he continues to be one of the most successful people in Hollywood. He continues to work hard and deliver project after project with consistency. He's a strong believer in invocation and thought processes. He once said in an interview that 2+2 is not 4, he said that in his reality 2+2 is whatever he wants it to be. Do you understand this concept? It wasn't about the actual math of, if you have two apples and you add another two apples you have four apples. It wasn't about that at all. What he was saying was, he controls his universe. He declares what things are and what things are not, he is deliberate, he is defiant he says what he believes is true. He is saying that when he speaks the universe will get out of his way. He's using his voice as creative power. The famous Martial Artist and Actor Bruce Lee once said, "Be like water, making its way through cracks. Do not be assertive, be the object, and you shall find a way around or through it. If nothing within you stays rigid, things will disclose themselves. Empty your mind, become, shapeless, like water. If you put water into a cup, it becomes the cup. You put water into a bottle and it becomes a bottle. You put it in a teapot, he becomes the teapot. Now, water can flow or can crash. Be water, my friend." You can adapt to your life situation just like water, it doesn't have to be how it is right now you can flow and change like a river. Who told you reached your capacity that you reached your limits? Take the limits off of yourself, take the limits off of the universe, take the limits off of your creator. You were not made with limitations, so be limitless. You can go back to school, I don't care what age you are, your mind never stops learning. I bet you learned something new today! That's how our creator made you, he made you with unlimited potential, he created you with curiosities on purpose, he wanted you to seek him, seek wisdom and invoke his power and presence in your life. Our brain and heart are about 73 percent water, so water is a major part of our life, just like air and food. Therefore if Bruce Lee was saying to be like water in the way that it flows over and around any obstacles, could it be in his wisdom that he was also saying something even deeper? Could he also be saying use your brain, in your thought process always, but also use your heart. The brain is great for critical thinking and using it for analytical purposes, but the heart is what we use for compassion and thinking about people. I've worked with people who are so black and white they don't know, how to deal with people on a daily basis. They have zero compassion for people. You cannot be this way, for what you show people it will be shown back to you. The bible says, your blessings will be pressed down shaken together and overflowing. Trust that you were created for a bigger purpose, your time is coming and when you move like the water, nothing will stop you.

CHAPTER

The Haters

PEOPLE WILL WANT YOU to do well, just not better than them! The moment you cross over into success, you will begin to see an instate change in the way people treat you and talk to you. When you have the "You Can" attitude, people will hate you. You have to be prepared for the fact that everyone will not celebrate you. Everyone won't celebrate your new promotion at work. Everyone won't celebrate the graduation of your child. Everyone will not celebrate the fact that you overcame sickness, that you defeated the drug addiction. Some people will only be your friends as long as you were doing the same thing that they are doing. But once you stop doing what they're doing they will leave you, they will be nowhere to be found, they will not want to hang out with you anymore.

Once you start to achieve the success that you've been working so hard to get some people won't stay around, they won't understand why you can't hang out with them at the bar, why you can't go to the club, for a quick drink and that's ok. They weren't meant to understand your new goals and dreams. There comes a time when you grow up and mature and you realize that you only have a limited amount of time and the success that you want to achieve will only involve a small circle of people. Ask yourself who is in my circle today, the people that are really for me? No it's not your Facebook friends, or your Instagram friends, or your Snapchat friends those are not real friends. Those are mostly haters trying to look into your life to see what it is that you post, what it is that you eat, what it is that you do on a daily basis. Your real friends are the people that you have the phone numbers to that you can call on a daily basis and have real conversations with and they give you real meaningful advice and help when you need it. If you can call someone at two or three in the morning and ask them for a ride to the airport and they don't get mad and the take you to the airport with a smile on their face that, is a real friend. The fact is, you will have more haters than friends. It doesn't matter where you are, you can be at work, school, church. Haters are everywhere and you will see them wherever you go. The best example of the person who had the most haters was Jesus. When you think of the example of his life, he went out every day he did his best, he listened to people, he helped people, he healed people some people loved him, but more people hated him, because they didn't understand him. They didn't understand how could a man be so loving and compassionate towards his people. But not only his people all people, healing the sick wounded and those in pain. I always looked at it this way if Jesus Christ the son of God had people that hated him so much they wanted to kill him and he was perfect, how much more so will you and I have haters that want to do harm to us and we are imperfect. Jealousy, envy, greed are so prevalent in the world we live in today and social media makes it so easy to for people to be bullies and act tough behind a keyboard. You can overcome the hatred, the bullies. There have been many people who have committed suicide based on the bullying. They never got the chance to really understand how blessed they were, how they were only in a tough time for a season and that very soon it would all pass away. If you know someone that is going through a tough time, be a light for them, encourage them, lift up their spirits. Let people know that you are there for them and that you are there to help them through their time of need, you just might save a life. You have the ability to coexist with all people no matter their religion or beliefs and it is vital that you are able to do so if you plan on being successful, remember people are the ambassadors of wealth and knowledge. If you have had issues in the past with other people's races or religions, I say this respectfully, let it go and instead of being judgemental try to work with these people try to understand these people and have compassion in your heart. Maybe you were raised in a household with different beliefs or racial tensions. When we are born we don't see color in fact we don't see anything at first so to us when we do gain our vision everyone looks the same. But as we grow older we are taught prejudice, we are taught what races are and we begin to look at one another by the color of their skin. There have been many police shootings lately many protests and movements like black lives matter, while the saying is true, in my opinion ALL lives matter, no matter the color. I believe the reason people focus so much on the black lives matter movement is, more black men are murdered by police officers than any other race. This is why they are specifically focusing on the words black lives matter. But I also have to say this to my people of color black and brown people, we must do our part as well, sometimes you are the ones provoking these type of attacks, having drugs and weapons in your car getting involved in thefts and high-speed chases on the freeway putting your life and putting the officers life in danger. People of color have to do better, don't put yourself in dangerous situations to begin with. Let's focus more on educating ourselves and educating our children making sure that our young men go to work, Instead of hanging out with their homies, who want to do nothing more than run the streets and get into trouble. Upon his release from prison, I recall meeting and hanging out with one of the most famous drug dealer's in the world, that spent many years behind bars and made millions of dollars daily. He told me how he inspired to be a tennis player but came from a very poor environment so to make money he turned to selling drugs. He sold drugs all across the nation had a team of people that worked for him and became very successful at what he did. The drugs had infiltrated the entire black community and he was a great salesman, but he was selling the wrong product. So to all the drug dealers reading this book, if you can sell drugs, you can sell pharmaceuticals, you can sell books at the library, you can sell food at a restaurant, you can sell clothing at a clothing store or shoes at Footlocker and you could even run your own business. In order to sell drugs you have to be a businessman. You have to know how to get the word out about your product that's called, promotion and marketing. You have to know what your customers like and don't like you have to have good customer service. You have to know how much of the product you have in stock that's called inventory. If you know how to do all of these things why don't you have your own business an honest business something that the law doesn't have to stop you from doing. He made close to 600 million dollars and had everything. He owned many houses, hotels and cars he was a multimillionaire when he was at the top of his game before he got arrested and went to prison. Now that he is a freeman, He is still a businessman he writes books has a literacy program now and helps the community, he changed his perspective and he changed his life, he didn't let the haters stop him or the naysayers that said you'll never get out of prison, you will never be more than what you currently are. He defied the odds no one expected him to get out of prison after doing what he did but this is how life works, there are opportunities everywhere, sometimes we don't know where they will come from but they will come. Maybe you're in that situation today, in a situation where you feel that you are stuck in that you will never be able to be more than you are or stop from selling drugs. I recall when he and I were talking he said that he had all of this money, but he never learned how to read and that he did not learn how to read, until he went to prison. What am I saying? I'm saying it's never too late for you, it's never too late to learn to read to continue your education to stop whatever it is that you are currently doing that is bringing you down. Education is the key. There is a business person inside of you, with knowledge and skills that needs to be shared it's ok, you can let it out, haters can't stop you, use them as your motivation.

CHAPTER

13

Heart Of A Champion

I AM TIRED OF hearing people say, "I never win anything." Well, that depends on what you consider, winning really is. You win every time you open your eyes in the morning, every foot step you're able to take unassisted, every time you hear a child's laughter. I think we need to redefine what true winning is. You may have not won a championship trophy, but that is not what this is about. You are winning in the game of life! Inside of you beats the heart of a champion. You need to be courageous enough, to let it out. You need to have the hunger, that Rocky Balboa mentality, that you will never give up and never give in! I had this same conversation with my daughter this morning. As I was driving her to school this morning, I told her, I expect you to be number one in your class. She asked, why? I said because you're a very smart girl and I expect you to do great things. I expect you to be number one in math, number one in reading, and number one in sports. I told her you come from a great line of champions and winners, we expect you to continue what we started. She's only eight years old, but why did I do this? I am planting a heart of a champion seed in her mind. She then put her head up, and walked straight into class ready to tackle anything that was thrown her way. I bet she gets an A+ on her test today. I keep telling her how great she is, how smart she is, and I know by planting these seeds she will remember these things for life. What seeds are you planting in the people around you today? I want my kids to be strong young ladies. I open the door for them, and hold their hand when we walk down the street, not all the time, but I try to remember. I want to be the kind of man, my girls aspire to marry some day. I want them to marry a God fearing man, with a great job, so he can provide for their family. Not too much to ask for, right? I want them to find a champion! I have seen many young ladies settle for less than their value, and end up with someone not worth their time or energy. But sometimes you must go through it, to grow through it. It's part of life, the hurts and pain, the breakups. Be a rubber band and bounce right off that person, get your fire back, take back your championship title. Winning is a mindset, do you see yourself as a winner or a loser? What name do you respond to? I will never forget playing Varsity for my high school basketball team at Paramount High School, and we had a game against the best high school team in the nation, Dominquez High School. Our coach, Coach Stewart, said this, "Tonight you'll be playing against future NBA players, don't expect to win!" In fact, don't even expect to come close to winning, tonight your goal is to not get dunked on and end up in the newspaper! I thought to myself wow, these guys must be superstars, and sure enough they were! The ball was tipped and on the very first play of the game our center got dunked on, by none other than, Tayshuan Prince. There were a lot of dunks that night and by the end we lost 135-28. We hold the record for the biggest game lost in school history, and the next morning our center made the front page of the newspaper, getting dunked on. We were happy we got to even play against those guys, we didn't care we lost. Our coach had zero confidence in our abilities because he knew, this school scouted out of state, and out of the country for the best players in the world! We were just a bunch of local kids from the neighborhood who could play the game. I think they even had a red headed kid on their team from Australia, how they made that happen, I'll never know. I actually appreciate our coach, being honest with us right from the start of the game. He knew this would not be a fairy tale underdog story. Our tallest player was 6'2, their tallest player was 7'2. Overage team height was 5'9, theirs was 6'7. It was truly David vs. Goliath, only this time Goliath step and dunked all over David. The coach set our expectations for us, after I had time to think about it, he was right. The only thing we could do, was go out there and do our best, we were going up against professionals, the goal was not to win, but to enjoy the show! These guys were flying through the air, doing tricks like the Harlem Globetrotters. It was a great sight to see. There will be winners and losers in life, that's just how life is, but how you react to those losses, will dictate your future. I can't think of anyone who likes to lose. No one wakes up and says, "I can't wait to be a real loser today!" "I am not going to do anything all day but sit at home, be a total loser and do absolutely nothing"! If that is your idea of enjoyment or success, you need to try something new. When you have the heart of a champion you know how to receive. Never be too proud to receive if your friend offers to buy you dinner, let them. If you see a coin on the street stop and pick it up no matter how small it is never be too proud to receive. If someone gives you a gift, receive it no matter how useless you may think it is, say thank you and receive it you can always regift it to someone else later. When you do these things you are telling the universe that your heart is open to receive, the universe does not know the difference between a penny and $1 million dollars, so when it's your turn to receive that large prize or large gift it will be huge. I like to call it "blocking your blessings". I never turn down anything that is given to me as a gift. If I see a penny on the street I will bend down and pick it up. I want to show that I'm not too proud and that money, even a small coin when collected becomes very valuable. Never deny your blessings because if you do you prevent yourself from getting more. Never feel bad about being blessed either or allow people to make you feel bad about your new blessings. Never feel bad about the new car, new baby, new house, new promotion at work, whatever it is receive it and don't allow others to make you feel anything less than blessed. Life is not fair, and also favor is not fair, either. You may wonder why the same people get promoted or catch many good breaks in life. Like the people who win the lottery twice, yes there are many people who have done so, but your attitude should not be why do they always win? Why do they always get promoted? Why do good things only happen to those people? The attitude you should have is celebrating their win! Show that you're not jealous or envious of them. You already know your blessing is right around the corner. We should not ask those questions we should be more focused on ourselves and the good things that are coming our way. By focusing on the blessings of others, it actually makes us very negative people because are more focused on their life than your own. So your next-door neighbor got a huge promotion and you have not yet, so what your time will come be patient and have faith. You will be blessed just as they have been blessed you're due season is coming you have not missed out on your opportunity just be patient. I know it's very hard for you and I to have this type of mentality, but we must do it. Just remember everything happens for a reason the good things you have done the things that you have built and accomplished will not go unnoticed and at the right time you reach new levels of success, I guarantee it. Have you ever wondered why things didn't happen when you wanted them to? A lot of the times it's because our Creator knows that we would not be able to handle it at that exact moment. When we ask for something there are always three answers yes, no and wait. Most of the time when you ask for something the answer is wait, and the reason for that is, you were not ready to receive it. Imagine if you asked for $1 million dollars right now and like magic, you were given it instantly. Do you already have a plan of what you would do with the money? I can almost guarantee you said Yes! You probably said, you would buy this, you would buy that, you would help this person, you would buy property, you would invest in this and so on and so forth. Action speaks louder than words and once that money goes into your bank account and you see all those zeros on your bank statement unless you have financial training you will start to have different feelings. The first place you'll end up if not the car dealership, is the mall. That is the reality of a person with a large sum of new money and zero financial planning. After you have some fun at the mall, then you may buy yourself a new car, most people focus on buying a new car before they buy a new house. The mind is totally backwards and we think of the fun new car before we think of shelter over our head. This is why you see a lot of our new pro athletes go broke after only a few years and waste millions of dollars buying things that they don't need and squandering their wealth on things that have no value. It's because we are not taught that when we are much younger and don't learn the value of a dollar or financial management or planning strategies. The school systems don't teach financial literacy. I was taught a very basic understanding of economics in high school and it really does not educate you enough to know what you need to know as you begin adulthood. The reality is that in the senior year of high school kids need to be taught about credit and how credit scores and credit usage affects them and will follow them the rest of their life. The moment you begin college you begin to get offered loans and credit cards many things that put you in debt forever and most people simply do not have the education or financial knowledge to be able to handle that new credit card. We know that credit scores are very important. They dictate what kind of interest-rate you get when you buy a car or get a mortgage and it follows you your entire life. This is very crucial information that I believe should be taught at an early age so you can learn to be financially responsible, but it starts with the right education and the right planning. Our country is full of millions of people that took out loans just to pay for college. You tried to better yourself by paying a high price for education, only to put yourself thousands of dollars in debt, and then find no job upon graduation. This is the struggle that many people face today. The good news is, no matter your situation, you must keep pursuing your education and in the end, it will pay off. You have the heart of a champion, so consider it all joy when you meet with various trails, keep working it will turn around.

CHAPTER

The People Around You

EVERYTHING IS NOT ALWAYS as it seems. There are some people around you that are specifically looking to do you harm and cause trouble. You know exactly who they are. They are the nosey next-door neighbors, the people who are trying to look into your life and see what it is that you are doing, the people, that have nothing better to do than focus on your life. The battle is not always yours to fight. You can let God be your vindicator! Let go and let God. Someone owes you money, a lot of money, let go and let God handle the matter. You were wronged in a business deal, your parents weren't there for you, your spouse left you, no matter the situation let go and let God. This is very difficult for some. I know that it used to be for me. I couldn't understand how someone could just let something go without getting revenge. It took me a very long time to learn that the battle is not mine, but I had to allow God to take care of it for me. This alleviated a lot of unneeded and unnecessary stress off of my life. When we let it go, all the burden and guilt is released from us. When we have been done wrong to by someone it's very easy for us to come up with all sorts of evil thoughts and ways of paying them back or seeking revenge and all the things that we could do to them, but if we really think about it, if we really did get our revenge where would it lead us to? Would it be prison? Would it be death? What would we lose or gain by doing this? There is an old expression that says, "Two wrongs don't make a right." We know that this expression is very true. The money that you are owed for the pain and suffering that you have received, when you try to pay someone back for what they did wrong to you, it will only leave you empty and broken. Why not go about it a different way? Why not try to meditate, calm down and relax or pray to God and ask for strength, strength with your attitude, for a clean mind and a clean heart. Too many times we want to settle the score and get even or do things our way but that's not the right approach to have. If you think this is the only way, then often times you will end up doing more harm than good. You have to be able to step back and think, think about all the things that you would lose. This is why it is never a good idea to make decisions when you're angry or upset because you will make the wrong choices. You have to make wise decisions, you cannot only think of yourself but must think about your family and the people who care about you the most and need you in their lives. When you think of others before yourself you begin to make better choices better decisions. Your children need you in their life, your brothers and sisters need you in their life, your spouse needs you in their life the community, the world needs you. You're very valuable to those around you and they appreciate what you do. Never think for one second that you are not valuable and never forget all the things that you do and all the people that you help on a daily basis. I asked one of my daughters to name one thing that they appreciate about me and she said, "I appreciate that you go to work Dad." I thought to myself wow, she actually notices Monday through Friday, I get up shower put my clothes on and go to work not for myself but for the family. She's only six years old and she noticed probably one of the most important things that I do as a father every single day. You are noticed everyday, and what you do makes a difference. It's a proven fact that people hate Mondays, why? It's because it's the first day of the week and for most the first work day of the week. So that means it's back to the grind, back to the drawing board, back to face the boss which means most people hate Mondays. However Friday is much different. Friday is the last day of the work week so people typically love Fridays. For most people it's also payday so that makes Fridays even better. Studies have shown that people are 10 times happier on Friday. It definitely makes sense when you look at both of those days but it really is up to you how you view them determines how you feel on those days. A positive outlook will carry you through the week until you reach "Happy Friday." You've seen it before or maybe in the movie, "The Office" when they say, "You've got a case of the Mondays." Try to look at Monday's differently from now on and say to yourself, "I will have a great day, I will be positive and things will work out for my good." Your attitude will make the day positive and productive. When you have a bad day or tough day at the office or school, do you carry that burden with you for the rest of the week? Do you have a revenge mindset that whatever bad thing happened on Monday you'll make sure to get that person or boss back on Tuesday or Wednesday or Thursday? You must possess the ability to quickly let it go and move on. There will be more opportunities to do better throughout the week and throughout the year. We are not born with this revenge mentality but when our feelings get hurt or someone says something to us that is out of context you're so quick to retaliate. A lot of the retaliation has to do with how we process information how we think and our patience. I love patient people. They can stay calm, cool, collected for a very long time in fact there so calm, that it's scary. What do I mean by that? I mean that you could make a patient person very angry but the fact that they are so calm about it is scary, because you have no idea what's running through their mind. They could be thinking the most absolute best plan in the world to pay you back while smiling in your face at the same time and you would have no idea. Being a patient person is a powerful thing. Knowing how to pick your battles is also a powerful thing. There is no need for you to get involved in every conversation or every fight that you hear because every battle is not worth your time. You may often hear disagreements as you're walking around the office or even at home but you should be careful what you lend your ear to, and what you get involved with and if it does not specifically involve your life then it should be none of your business let it go. There are a lot of nosy people who love to get involved in everything and things that have no business with them or their family but yet want to know every single detail of the story, the gossip. Stay away from those people. Those are the people that you cannot trust with any information. You know who they are in your family at your school and in the office. You tell them one thing and they go off and tell 10 other people and that's just how they are. The fastest way to spread miss truth is with the person who likes to gossip. I love this one joke I heard it involved three Pastors who were out on the boat fishing and one of the Pastors said to the other two, "We never let our hair down and talk about the things that bother us so I'd like for each of us to share our biggest sin with one another, just one thing." The first Pastor said, "I have trouble with gambling, I like to play sometimes on the weekends." The second Pastor said, "Well I have trouble with paying taxes I don't always pay them." But the third pastor was very hesitant but finally he said, "My biggest trouble is with gossip and I can't wait to get off this boat." You have to be careful who you give your information to, who you lives close to you, because they might be like the third Pastor, always talking about someone else. There is a saying that says, Big minds talk about creative things, small minds talk about people. No matter what you do people will talk about you, they will talk good and they will talk bad, they will talk gossip and make up stories but if they're talking about you that only proves that you are a very interesting person because people with no lives love to talk about people who are full of life so congratulations on that! I hope people talk about you all the time. I hope you are the topic of their every conversation because that means that you're successful. The more haters you have the more successful you are. It's an odd concept to grasp. People don't talk about people who are doing nothing, people talk about people that they want to be like. They may not admit it to you but they look up to you, they look up to your children, they look up to your spouse, your job, your car, your cat, your dog, whatever it is that you have that is working for you they want it. You're surrounded by people who are for you and people who are against you all the time, never forget that. A good friend of mine just started his own business and people were very surprised at the fact that he was able to do it by himself. But once he got it up and running it became very successful now everyone in his outer circle wanted to be in his inner circle, why is that? People are attracted to success. They want to be a part of something more than themselves so if you are the successful one of your group of friends they will attach themselves to you, like a magnet. This is very dangerous because some people will want to attach themselves to you and have nothing to bring to the table nothing to offer to your business or your life those are the ones you need to cut off immediately because they will become like a sponge sucking up whatever it is that is around you and try to make it their own. It's true there is power in numbers but when it comes to success and people those numbers should be limited. You cannot take everyone with you on the path to greatness. Your main concern should be your closest family members and close friends. You also cannot be afraid to change. Steve Harvey once ran into a young man at one of the movie studios and the young man expressed an interest to work for Steve Harvey. The young man had long dreadlock style hair and Steve Harvey told ask him how long have you had that type of hair? The young man looked at him and said, "All of my life I've never cut it." Steve Harvey then said, I go to a lot of meetings with CEOs and high-powered people if I take you in the meeting with me what will those people think of me? The young man stated I've never really thought about that. Steve Harvey was not trying to say that the young man style was bad, but what he was saying was if you want to be in my inner circle of people you must look as presentable as I do. The next week the young man ran into Steve Harvey again at the same studio and he went up to Mr. Harvey and said, "do you recognize me?" Steve Harvey had to look at him up-and-down because he did not recognize the young man, the young man had cut all of his hair off. The young man went on to tell Steve Harvey that he wished that he had cut his hair off a long time ago. He went on to say people are now stopping him to have conversations he even got offered a couple of jobs because he was so clean-cut. He thanked Mr. Harvey for his advice and told him that his advice was life-changing. To me this story is very powerful it goes to show that if you want something you have to be willing to change and if you want to be around certain people or in certain circles you must be willing to change. When you are willing to change people look at you differently just like this young man. He was so used to having that look and he thought it was fine and yes there is nothing wrong with having long hair, but sad to say some people don't understand men with long hair or the attention that it brings. Steve Harvey was trying to show this man that if he wanted to be around him then he would have to be as sharp as Steve is. We all know that Steve Harvey dresses very professional has very groomed hair and mustache so he wants people that are in his circle to mirror his image of professionalism he selects the people the people don't select him. Are you sharp today? Are you professional? Do the people in your inner circle reflect the person that you are or the person that you want to be? That answer should be yes!

CHAPTER

15

Growing Pains

You NEED TO BE like a pregnant lady right now! You need to be uncomfortable, a little scared, tired and ready to give birth. Ready to give birth to your dreams. We need to make sure you a ready and that your contractions are getting closer and closer. You love to be comfortable! Waking up every day in the same old bed, next to the same old wife/husband, waking up the same old kids, to eat the same old breakfast, to take them to the same old school, in your same old car, then you're on your way to the same old job, to see the same old boss, and same old co-workers, getting ready to eat the same old lunch, work on the same old assignments, then end your day driving back to your same old house, then eat your same old dinner, then back to your same old bed. Sound Familiar?

I just summarized your entire day, or some variation of it. The hamster wheel syndrome that most people are on day in and day out. Many years ago, when I was in the eighth grade I had a teacher who assigned us the task of making a vision board. If you've never done it, I suggest you make one. Get a cardboard and, a glue stick and glue all the things you want to attract to your life on that board. You fill up the board with pictures of all the things that you would like to achieve and then you post it somewhere in your home or office or all around your house so you can visually see it every day and recall what you're working towards. Having a constant reminder around you is very powerful and very motivational. There are many people today even celebrities like Oprah Winfrey who do these things. If you don't have a vision or know where you're going you will go nowhere. Your thoughts must be aligned with your vision. You must continue to think about what is on your vision board throughout the day. Encourage your family, your friends, your coworkers to do the same and surround yourself with other visionary people and keep them in your inner circle. Get together with them and talk about your goals dreams and aspirations. Make regular meetings to keep each other encouraged and on the right path. There are people just like you in the world that want more, that want to succeed. I speak weekly and give encouraging presentations to my team of like-minded individuals. I am involved in the sales world and this year our goal was to make $1 million dollars and we did it by November 30TH. Yes that one million dollars was on my vision board. It didn't come easy, there were a bunch of bruises along the way. There were days we made hardly anything and then there were some exceptional days and some record-breaking improvement days. You have to be able to roll with the punches and expect the unexpected along the way. The journey that you are on is an exceptional one not meant for everyone. Sometimes you will have to travel alone and have many sleepless nights while you focus on your goal. Not only planning out your vision through your vision board but actually believing that you can achieve it is very important. Yes, you will have doubters and people that won't understand your vision and that's just fine. You have your vision and they have their own. What is meant to be for you, will be for you and what is meant to be for them will be for them. Success should be on your mind constantly. Thoughts of winning, thoughts of victory. While everyone else around you will have what if's and thoughts of lack in their mind, you will have the opposite thoughts. Don't allow the negativity of not having what is on your vision board now, get you discouraged. Remember your vision board is a future forecast it is not the things that you have now, they are the things that you would like to work for or work towards achieving. The more elaborate your vision board the more work you will have to put into achieve those goals. If you put a picture of a yacht or a picture of a $10 million dollar home on your vision board unless you fall into some giant windfall it will take some time in order to achieve those dreams or goals. We have all thoughts of winning the lottery and all the cool and exciting things that we could do with that money, but unless that type of money falls into your lap, it's going to take some work and some ideas to get you there. I believe that you have the capability to do it as long as you stick to your plan specifically your action plan and never waiver or doubt yourself, you can achieve anything. It starts with your vision and it must be clear, it must be direct, but most importantly you must believe in it. Push forward create your vision board today and start pressing towards your dreams. You cannot afford to wait for things to come your way, you must take action if you want to see any type of results. We all need a vision and we all need encouragement. The truth is none of us can reach your highest potential by ourselves. We need one another and you can be the one that stirs up seeds of greatness for someone else and sparks a new idea. The word encourage simply means to, "urge forward" everyone of us should have someone we believe in, someone we're urging forward someone we're helping to achieve goals. Hall of Fame baseball player Reggie Jackson once said, "A great manager has the ability to make a player think that he's better than he is. He convinces you to have confidence in yourself. He let's you know that he believes in you, and before long you discover talent that you never knew you had." This is what happens when someone believes in you and your vision. I do this often with people around me. I do this with my kids, I let them know that they are the best kids, the smartest kids, the number one kids on the planet. Just planting seeds in them before the world does, before the world tries to convince them that they are something that they are not, they already know that they're great, they already know that they are more than champions every day. I tell them this on our morning drive to school before they get out of the car, I remind them that they are winners, that they are champions, that they are very intelligent. I make sure before they get out of the car that they are loaded up and they are fully encouraged, they are ready to conquer the world. How would the world be today if all parents did that to their children? Give them the vision, give them hope and the opportunity to succeed. My children already know I expect nothing less than the best from them. I don't care if they are playing soccer or taking a math test, to me it is all the same. When you do your best and believe in yourself the best is sure to follow. I let them know I can only encourage you to do your best but it's up to you to follow through. I can't take the test with you and I can't be on the field when you play your game, but I can be your number one supporter, your cheerleader from the sidelines and that I will always be there. You may have a vision that is giving you growing pains but you still need a boost of confidence. The brilliant carmaker Henry Ford, got his confidence boost from the brilliant inventor, Thomas Edison. Henry Ford got introduced to Thomas Edison as the man who was trying to build a car that ran on gasoline. When Thomas Edison heard this he got excited slammed his fist on the table, and said, "You've got it! A car that has its own power plant that's a brilliant idea." Up to that point Henry Ford had so many negative people saying bad things against him that he had started to think that his idea to build a car was a bad idea. A simple vote of confidence gave him the boost that he needed and urged him to keep pressing forward to keep pursuing his dream. Now look at where Ford motor company is today. We all need someone to believe in us more than we believe in ourselves to see our potential, to look ahead and enlarge our vision. When you help people expand their thinking you help them grow a real vision for their life. Be a booster for others, people are scared enough as it is to go after what they really want, you can be the difference maker. You can help them give birth to the dreams they need. Some people are scared to tell you their vision. They don't want to get laughed at or ridiculed they don't want people making fun of their dreams so they keep their dreams in a little box inside of their head too scared to share it, too scared to go after it. Don't let that be you today. Who cares what other people think? Who cares what other people have to say? This is the mentality that you need to have. You have to be strong enough in your mind and in your actions that no matter what any other person may think or say you will pursue your dreams. They may laugh at you they may think you're crazy but you know what you have to do, it's been growing inside of you for so long, has it been six months? Has it been nine months? Has it been a few years? With your vision, and with your action plan, and with faith in yourself it's time to give birth. Just breathe and focus on what you want. People do not decide your destiny, you do, now is the time for you to turn your growing pains, into growing profits.

CHAPTER

16

You Can Celebrate

You must know when to stop and smell the roses! You get so caught up in the work, and planning stages of your goals and dreams that you are driving along the road and you don't realize you have gone an extra five miles and already past your destination. I am sure you have used a navigation system as you have driven before. When you past your destination, what does the navigation voice say? Does she say, "Hey loser, you missed your turn back there!" No! She says, "Recalculating." She's not mad at you, she's not talking down to you, she simply says recalculating to find a better route and then guides you along the way. Too many times we think I missed up I made a mistake and that we can't recalculate our own lives that we can't celebrate ourselves our successes. But just like the navigation we have to be able to tell ourselves I messed up, but I'm recalculating, I'm getting myself back on track. Doing that is reason to celebrate yourself and when you create some more wins and you achieve those wins, you can celebrate your successes along the way. Think about what it is that you can celebrate today. Did you start a new diet? Did you follow the diet? Have you lost weight? Have you looked for a job today? Did you even apply? Did you wake up before the alarm clock went off today? I am sure there is something that you did today that is worth celebrating and if you have nothing yet, today is still here, and tomorrow is another opportunity. Every day I hear people saying that they want to accomplish this or accomplish that but the question is, what are you doing to achieve it? And when you do accomplish something no matter how small it is don't forget to complement yourself. The late great basketball genius John Wooden once told his players, "After you score a basket, always look for the player who made the pass to you and acknowledge them. Nod your head. Smile. Point your finger. Do something that expresses your appreciation for the assist." One of the player said, "What if he's not looking?" John Wooden replied, "Don't worry he'll be looking." The point is we all love to be celebrated, we all love to be appreciated and to feel valued. You have to be able to look back on the past accomplishments and draw inspiration from them and stay focused on the encouraging thoughts. You have to be able to replay your celebrations, replay your victories and know deep inside of you that God did not bring me this far to leave me here if he did it for me in the past, he'll do it for me again in the very near future. You can get your joy back very fast if you're willing to change the channel in your mind. Maybe God gave you the house. I remember when my family didn't have a house and we stayed with family. I'm not ashamed to say that. Everything in my life was not always wonderful there was plenty of struggle and plenty of lack. I recall driving past a house, in a nice neighborhood that had a sign in front of it and thought to myself quickly, how nice it would be to live in that house. I remember coming home that day so excited to tell my wife and kids that I had found us a house and if we could go drive by and check it out. They agreed and that night we went to go look at the house. We must've sat outside in front of that house for about two hours just envisioning the house as our own, talking about where we would put our furniture and how we would decorate it. The only problem was the house was not ours. So we decided to pray and we prayed over the house and we prayed over the current owners of the house and we prayed that the house would become ours. For the next two weeks we would drive to the house park our car in front of the house and in the driveway and we would pray over the house, praying that house, it would eventually become ours. I bet the neighbors probably looked out of the window and thought there goes that crazy family again, I wonder why they keep coming to the house and spending time in front of the house every single night? We were doing something. We were planting the seed. We knew that it was not ours yet, but we had faith and we believed. Finally the day came where we met with the owner and the owner told us to flat out there were about 15 families ahead of us, that have priority over us, I don't think you will get this home. I didn't believe those lies, not for one second, when you truly believe in something and you truly want something to happen there is nothing that will stop you. We filled out all the papers anyway and we begin to plan and build and pray over what we wanted every single day for the next month. Then one day I got a call while I was at work saying that the house would be ours. I will never forget calling my family with tears in my eyes to tell them that we will be moving out of our family's house and moving into our own home. We literally put all of our faith and every prayer power we had into that house. There is no way we should have beat out 15 other families for the house, we didn't stand a chance. Logically, logistically, we should still be looking for a house but I believe God had another plan he had another idea for our family. We gave everything we had to him. We trusted him and we believed that he would move mountains and that he would turn things around in our favor and he did. What am I saying? I am saying that you can do the same. I don't know what it is that you're hoping for. Maybe you are in a similar situation today you're looking for a home for your family as I was. You're looking for a new job, a better job, as I was. Let me tell you I've been there and done that. I've been in your shoes, I know what it's like, to not know where your next meal will come from or where you will live next month. You have to go through it, to grow through it. Once you do you can always look back and you can always have something to celebrate and be grateful for, proud of. Sometimes I just stand outside of our house and I still get teary eyed. I realize and appreciate where I came from, where I am now in life the people who tried to close the doors of opportunities to me and my family, the people that did not want to allow us to be in their neighborhood and how we live in a better neighborhood then they could ever imagine. I remember those days and I appreciate those days, because now I can appreciate my right now, the season that I'm in and so can you. I don't live in some mega mansion with acres and acres of land I appreciate and I celebrate the home that God has blessed myself and my family with. When you appreciate the blessing that God has given you, you open the door for more blessings. You have to become a person that knows how to celebrate and appreciate the things that you have been blessed with. I guarantee you have many things that you can celebrate right now, things that happened to you in the present and in the past. The time you were in that legal battle and he made it out with flying colors. The time you were in the hospital and you made it out of that situation better than before. The time you thought you were going to fail that test and you ended up with a higher score than you thought you could never achieve. The time you prayed for a miracle and you received it. Things do not always happen when we want them to, but they always happen when they're supposed to. Do you have a reason to celebrate? You always do! Remember that this is gradual, this is progress not perfection. You are a work in progress, and you deserve to celebrate. Remember the good things that have happened in your life, and you will be filled with faith.

CHAPTER

Blessed

CREATE A BLESSINGS FILE! Everyday write down five things, that you have been blessed with. Here's an example. Today, I am blessed, I woke up, I am able to walk and talk. I am blessed to have a job. I am blessed that I have a home to stay in. I am blessed to have good health. I don't know about you but I feel better already! When you start your day with the blessings, you will end your day with blessings. Are you beginning your day with curses? Try to refrain from using curse words as much as you can. This might be hard for you. Maybe your parents used curse words all day long. Maybe you were taught nothing but bad words. Can I tell you they are called curse words for a reason. When you say them, you are calling in bad things to happen to you. You are drawing in the evil spirits to sit right next to you. I don't know about you, but I don't want any part of that in my life. It hurts me when I hear young children say curse words, I can only imagine who they learned those words from. They learned them from the parents, relatives or nearby friends in school. My parents didn't always use the best words, so when I went to school, I learned every curse word possible, and since my school was seventy percent Spanish, I even learned every bad word in Spanish too. Back then I was proud of that, I would even practice my expressions saying the curse words, I wanted the words to roll off my tongue with ease, kind of how comedians, say them like Katt Williams and Kevin Hart. I was young and foolish, and I didn't realize I was bringing in negative energy around me at the time. I made friends with other people who spoke the way I did, and there I was, a fourth grader with a potty mouth. Just like those South Park kids on T.V. we were those kids, but in real life. We learn as we grow up, just like everything in life. How can you expect to live a blessed life, if you only speak bad words? It won't work, you cannot have it both ways. Either you are blessed or you're not. Continue to speak the blessings over your life. When someone asks, "How are you today?" Say, "Blessed and you?" Never say, "I feel sick, I feel weak or tired." You might actually feel that way, but vocalizing it, only increases that feeling, so switch it up. People might come up to you and say you look sick. Say, "No I feel great, I am not claiming that sickness over me!" I recall a female co-worker eating a salad in the break room, and one of the negative females in the office came up to her and asked, "Aren't you married? Why are you eating a salad?" I love the way the co-worker eating the salad responded. She said, "I am eating salad, for me, I want to be healthy, for myself, not for my husband." The co-worker who asked the question was very bitter. She was a single, middle aged mother of a son, who had been through a tough divorce. She was a trouble maker at work and no one really liked her. The day she quit the office threw a celebration that she found a new job. Her leaving the company was a blessing to so many people, including her supervisor. She didn't understand that her negativity, only impacted herself no matter how hard she tried to put her bad attitude on others, it never worked, and she knew it. Let those people say what they want, they will never be happy, and they will never succeed. Guess what she will do? She will take her bitterness to the next company and the next until no one will want to put up with her attitude. She didn't see, the blessings in her own life, which hindered her spirit. She didn't recognize the fact that she was healthy, that she had a very talented and healthy son, that she had a job, a place to stay and food on her table. She didn't recognize all of the blessings that were surrounding her. But instead she chose to focus on everyone else around her, her coworkers their lives and was more concerned with being at the bar then focusing on her dreams. This is very easy for people to do when they don't recognize their blessings, gifts and talents they tend to focus on all the negative things in life. Ask yourself am I being a blessing or am I hindering the people around me? Hopefully you answer that you are a blessing and that when people come in contact with you they feel better, they feel uplifted, they feel encouraged. There is enough negativity in the world the people that you're around don't need any more added to it. So ask yourself another question who have I blessed today? There are many people around you right now that need to hear some good news from you. Be mindful however there is a major difference between blessing someone and someone taking advantage of you, let me explain. It is not your job to bless the same person every single day. If someone is constantly asking you for money, help or anything that takes you away from your normal day you are not blessing them, they are simply taking advantage of you. You have to have balance and you have to know when to cut it off. I have seen many situations where people ask for help but then continually ask for help just a few days later. I learned a funny principal from Steve Harvey he said due to his success a lot of his family members often call him and ask him for many things. So when they call his cell phone he waits a full 48 hours before he returns there call because he knows that they are about to ask him for something. So when he calls that person that called him 48 hours later, they tell him they already figured it out, I already solved that issue. He said people should be able to figure out what they were going to do without getting you involved and without calling you for help. There's nothing wrong with helping your family members and loved ones but let's face the facts, we all know who of our family and friends are always calling asking for something and the best thing you can do for them is make them independent people, that is their blessing. Don't be afraid to say No and mean it. You can love your family, but it is not your job to be at their every call to do everything that they need you to do, sometimes they simply need to figure it out all on their own. Do you bless the homeless? I grew up in Los Angeles and I've walked through the heart of skid Row in downtown Los Angeles where there are thousands of homeless people. In Los Angeles not too far from the Staples Center near many affluent businesses, is extreme poverty. I have a habit of not carrying cash or coins, usually I have a debit card on me, so when a homeless person asks for money I usually am not able to give them anything, unless at that moment I happen to have a few dollars in my pocket or coins I'll give it to them and pray with them. You'd be surprised how many of them welcome a prayer more than money. When I see a homeless person in the distance as I am driving or wherever I go, I close my eyes and say a quick prayer over them. They don't know it, but I know I did my part to bless them. I pray for them to be blessed, for their healing, for them to find shelter and food. Even if they aren't a believer, that doesn't matter to me. You have to do, what you believe is right. I have seen people healed and delivered immediately after being prayer for, prayer is powerful. It doesn't matter if you know them or not, you can bless a stranger today. That's exactly what Jesus did, everywhere he went he healed the sick and spoke the blessings over people and most of them, he had just met physically. Don't discriminate your powerful blessings, give them away freely. You have had people pray for you that you don't even know. Your mother and father, your grandmother, your church members have all said prayers over your life. The Bible says when two or more are gathered in his name, that's when things start to happen. Have you ever been in a prayer circle? That is when two or three people hold hands and they all pray over a specific thing together. There is power in that group of words, when you speak the blessings together, you come in agreement over a specific topic, then soon enough your healing, your blessings will come. When you speak it, you will receive it!

CHAPTER

18

Nice Guys Finish First

IN BUSINESS, THERE IS an idea that if you're nice and compassionate towards people, you will always get stepped on, or taken advantage of. I think our world portrays that the boss or leader must be extra tough or rough with the people they lead in order to earn respect. I disagree with this thought process. In order to be a leader you have to be able to serve. You have to be able to work with people of all races and backgrounds, without letting your personal feelings get in the way of business. We are taught that nice guys finish last, that if you're a man, you must be mean in everything you do. Men today aren't taught joy, to smile or laugh, they are taught to be more serious. You need to know as a man, it's ok to smile, laugh, and cry. Men tend to hide their real emotions. Try not to take yourself so seriously all the time, learn that there is a time for everything. Remember also to keep your peace in all things. Yes there will be things that will make you frustrated and mad, when things don't appear to go your way, but you have the power to keep your peace. Men may not admit it, but we are emotional creatures like women. I grew up watching WWF wrestling people like, Hulk Hogan, Macho Man Randy Savage, The Ultimate Warrior, these were my early heroes. These were all tough guys. Guys that would deal out punishment week after week, they were strong and showed no weakness. I recall saying to myself at a very young age, I would love to be a pro wrestler. I am so glad I never stuck to that plan because when I got older I started to understand the physical abuse that these men take. I give them a lot of credit for their craft and being able to entertain millions of people regardless of broken bones, bloody noses or physical strain that their body endures. I give a lot of credit to pro football players as well. We forget that they take similar abuse day after day and week after week even though they're wearing pads and helmets and now we are starting to see the true overall effects with concussions and other alements that follow football players for the rest of their life. I recently started to watch the sport of Rugby and I realized these are the toughest man of all they are running around tackling each other with absolutely no pads whatsoever. That takes a lot of guts and a lot of heart. Then I begin watching mixed martial arts or MMA fights and I learned a brand-new level of heart. These fighters must be strong willed and tough in the ring, but can I tell you, I have met a few outside the ring and they are some of the nicest people. You wouldn't even know, just the day before they were in a huge fight. Why is that? They are disciplined, they know how to turn it on and turn it off. They know when to be tough and when to be kind. They recognize the time and place for everything. Everything does not require an attitude, you don't have to wake up angry, however some people do. They wake up with a chip on their shoulder even before the day has begun. How do you wake up with an attitude while you're eating at the breakfast table? Can you really have an attitude while you're eating Fruit Loops or Lucky Charms? I doubt it. If you do wake up on the wrong side of the bed in the morning try to have a new approach, focus on the good things that are about to happen that day. You need to focus on being a nicer person, remember nice guys finish first. The only thing that having a negative attitude in the morning will bring you is more negative things throughout the day. When you begin to be nice, people around you will start to be nice. It's really a domino effect. Who enjoys being around angry frustrated people? I know I don't, so why become one of them? It doesn't cost anything to be kind, or lend help to someone in need. I promise that everything you do, is accounted for, and it will come back to you ten times more, so make sure you're putting out positive energy. There is a reason why the nice guy always wins in the movies, at the end of the story. The truth is no one likes the villain, no one ever wants evil to prevail. We hope that Superman, wins and saves the girl. We hope that all is right in the world and that everything turns around in our favor. I am sure you have tasted a Coca-Cola beverage before. Did you know that in their first year of business they only sold 400 drinks? That's right the entire year only selling 400 drinks. They could've easily had the attitude of we will never get this company off the ground so let's just shut our doors down now and save ourselves a lot of trouble. That would've been the easy way out, the quick fix. Fast forward many years later and the rest is history, they are now a multibillion-dollar worldwide company. They didn't give up, they didn't let a bad first year control their destiny. Maybe this year has been bad for you? Or maybe last year wasn't the most productive. You can be like Coca-Cola, you can keep going, not focus on the bad report, but stay focused on your product and believe in it and know that what you've created is very good. Coca-Cola understood the value of what they had and they knew if they kept going that dream would be successful. The problem you have is that you have a lot of things in your mind, a ton of ideas that you want to accomplish but you haven't truly decided on the one thing that you want to do. The reality is you can't be everything, you can't learn everything and you can't do everything, you must decide. Deciding is the first step to moving toward your goal it must be clearly defined. Your opportunity has been in your mind the entire time, but are you prepared and are you persistent? It's not always easy to keep the nice guy mentality, remember when you were driving the other day and that guy cut you off, almost caused you to get in an accident? Remember when you were at the grocery store walking to the checkout line and three people jumped in front of you? Remember when you lost your keys to your car, and you couldn't find them, now you have to pay 300 dollars for a replacement key? Remember when traffic was so bad, and you even left home extra early to make it to work on time, but you still ended up being ten minutes late? This is called life. The Bible says that the sun shines on the just and the unjust. Or in order words, the sun shines on the good guys and the bad guys, the same, but it's up to you to decide which team you want to be on. Try to be your best everyday and put a smile on your face regardless of the spilled coffee on your new dress, or the trash that the garbage man did not pick up, look at it from a blessed perspective. You're too blessed to be stressed, don't sweat the small stuff, look at the big picture, it gets better.

CHAPTER

Prepared By Persistence

How BAD DO YOU want success? You need to be persistent. The word persistent, is defined as continuing firmly or obstinately in a course of action in spite of difficulty or opposition. You need to be bold. You need to try more than once. You have to keep knocking on the closed doors and get creative. You need persistent faith. When you're persistent you will be blessed with more than what you asked for. When you knock on a door what happens? You must wait until someone answers. Right now you are standing at the door of opportunity knocking, but you must wait. If you don't hear anyone coming, knock again. There is an example in the Bible of a man who knocked on his neighbors door because a visitor came to his house and he wanted to give him some bread but the man had no bread. So the man with no bread knocked on his neighbors door and as he knocked, he asked for bread, but it was late and his neighbor was sleeping. So the man that needed the bread knocked but his neighbor would not answer, so he waited. When he did not hear anything he kept knocking, and knocking until finally his neighbor opened the door and he told him, please I have a visitor at my home and he is asking me for bread, but I don't have any. Can you please give me some bread so that I can give it to him so he can be on his way? He asked and he asked, he was very persistent until the neighbor who had bread went and grabbed much bread, gave it to the man and then he was on his way. We have to be persistent with our goals if we are not like this man, if we don't keep knocking on opportunities that we know are there, how can we expect to receive our bread or our goal? When you see small children in the store and they see a new toy that they want or a piece of candy, they ask their parents if they can get it. What do they do if the parent says no? They cry, they throw a fit right in the store especially very, very young children, they know the meaning of being persistent. No one had to teach them this behavior they simply see something that they want and if they don't get it, they will start to immediately be unhappy and cry. That is called persistence it's inside of you since birth, since they can't understand the concept of seeing something and not having it, they cry. Some people in your life you need to be persistent with. You can explain something to them over and over again and they still won't understand, you know who they are. You can make it as simple as possible you can draw them a picture, write them an email and they still don't understand. You can only do that for so long before you stop. You don't need to be persistent with a person who refuses to understand you, don't waste your time or energy. In your relationships you don't need to be persistent with a person who shows no interest in you, don't waste your time. Be persistent with the people who show interest in you and in your dreams. You may feel today like you have been persistent and things have still not turned out your way. That simply means you must keep knocking at the door that you must keep going because it's the persistent people that eventually make things happen for themselves. Nothing can stop you from making it happen but if you give up now, you will never know how far you could've gone or how successful you would have been. Every time that you failed was not a failure, it was a learning opportunity. You learned, you regrouped and you moved forward. Your setback was only a set up, you knocked at the door of opportunity, you attended the job interview, you attended the conference, you attended the meeting and nothing happened, don't you sit there and get discouraged because you didn't get an immediate answer, just wait. You are being prepared by your persistence. What does that mean? It means that your persistence, you taking that call, you attending that meeting or conference taught you the power of being patient. Everything will not happen on your timetable but it will happen if you stick with it. I have seen so many people give up on their dreams simply because it did not happen immediately or when they expected it to. If you do that, then it only shows that the dream was not really in you to complete. You gave up and the fact is many times we are only inches away from achieving what we want, but we get tired, w get frustrated, we give in to the doubt and the naysayers. What will it take for you to keep going and stay motivated? Always think of the final result, always envision the end is not far off. Develop patience, develop persistence, and develop prayer. Encourage yourself, talk to yourself, say this will not defeat me, I am getting stronger, I am getting smarter, my creative juices are flowing, I will not lose. I will be successful, my breakthrough is coming, it is right around the corner. Great things are about to happen to me! Maybe you've never done any of these things before, now is the time to begin. Saying these things helps you build your confidence muscles. When you work out in the gym, if you're trying to get bigger arms you lift weights that increase your bicep muscles. You need to spend hours, targeting that muscle group and you need to lift weights that you normally don't in order to increase your mass. It's the same way with your confidence muscles. If you've never worked out these muscles, the things that you say to yourself or the things in your mind, might be negative, start working out by saying the confident things over yourself, you'll be glad that you did. You'll start to see yourself as the person you want to be, prosperous, blessed, successful. You must be willing to not get down on yourself while you're in the waiting process you will go through seasons where it appears that absolutely nothing is going your way. You lost your job, your spouse left you, the kids have bad grades, you got into a car accident, and the dog ran away. Sounds like the perfect country song. Regardless of all of that, remember it's only a season of unfortunate incidents and they will pass away, maybe not today or tomorrow but things have a way of working themselves out over time. Stay patient, and know that the best is yet to come. Stay persistent, and keep after it, day by day. The only person that can keep you from your destiny is you, don't be the person that puts a halt to your victory. It's time to lace up the shoes and put on the big boy/big girl pants. You're in competition, not with your co-workers, family, friends or boss. The only competition, is within you. Can you be better today than yesterday? What is it going to take to challenge yourself to reach new levels? You've waited long enough, it's movement time. Now let that sink down into your spirit today. It's Movement Time! How will you move on your idea, that you didn't do yesterday? What will you do differently? What is going well? These are just a few of the questions you should be asking yourself as you're moving toward your project being complete.

CHAPTER

20

Relationship Mindset

YOU'VE HEARD THE EXPRESSION, "It's not what you know, but who you know." I agree with this statement to some degree. We have all seen "nepotism", which is the practice among those with power or influence of favoring relatives or friends, especially by giving them jobs. Having the inside track on jobs, or have a family member already a part of the business, sometimes does help. The other person might have more experience, or knowledge, but the fact that they don't have a relationship on the inside, forces them to lose. In order for you to be successful, you must have a relationship mindset. You must realize, you can't do everything on your own, and you need a strong team behind you, and a great relationship with everyone on your team. It starts with respect. Be honest, be human, don't pretend like you know it all and ask for help when you need it. Your team will appreciate the fact that you consider their thoughts and feelings, when making decisions, they will feel more a part of the team, when you lean on them at times for input. Consider the other person's communication style. I have worked with very silent people, who hardly spoke at all, and I have worked with extremely loud individuals, who shouted every word they spoke. You have to be understanding of their background. Perhaps they don't know, they speak so low that only an ant would be able to hear them. Perhaps they don't know, they're not at a football game, so they don't have to yell every word that they say to you. Every person you speak with will have a different communication style so it's up to you to adapt. When you have a relationship mindset you understand that it takes a solid effort to work on communication. The number one reason why most relationships don't last is because of poor communication. You thought she said one thing when she actually said another. You thought he said he would be in at 1 o'clock and he actually said 4 o'clock. There are so many variables when it comes to communication so speak slowly and clearly. Confirm that everyone understands you when you speak and keep it simple. If you don't understand what a person is trying to say don't be afraid to ask them to explain it again or take notes. Commit to making sure you have all the facts right. Your communication impacts the relationship. Think about the future. Think to yourself if this will be a future relationship and if it is, you know that there will be some investing involved in the relationship, so try to focus on the future. When you speak to people be purposeful, be deliberate and give an intentional message. But in order to do that you first must strategize and have a plan. You must be mindful, you must consider the other person's perspective what they might think as a possible idea or solution and then focus on the solution. You must be accountable and what that means is simply you must take responsibility for all of your actions take ownership of your idea and your team. Take responsibility if your project succeeds or your project fails, take responsibility. You might have to align with the person with whom you are communicating with or without being in total agreement. This happens all the time in business. You may have an idea that you think is truly great but your business partner may have a totally different mindset and they think it's a horrible idea and that's ok. You will not agree on everything that comes your way but you will work through it together as a team. Be sure to listen to your partners thoughts. Do more listening than talking and be understanding. Try to keep an open mind your way will not always be the best way and ensure that the message is received as intended and if it's not do your best to clarify their understanding. Remember that you are in a relationship so how you communicate is very important whether it is in person, email or telephone and never forget that your tone of voice will help or hinder the relationship. Remember it's not what you say, it's how you say it. This plays a very important role. You can say the words, "I hate you" with a straight face and then turn around and say the words, "I hate you" with a smile on your face and they will be treated very differently one will be taken as a serious remark and the other would be looked at as a joke. Why? It's not what you said, it's how you said it. Often times we say things that we don't mean and we come off as rude at home and in the workplace. So if that has happened how do you fix the broken relationship? You cannot take back words once they are said, but what you can do is be better, be kind the next time around and stay consistent with your kindness. Remember if you want to be successful you must remember to have a relationship mindset at all times these are the people that you are surrounded with day in and day out so you need to keep good relations with them remember a good relationship with people is like money in the bank so keep your account full. You never get another chance to make a first impression. Have you worked on your 15 second elevator pitch? Imagine you just walked into an elevator, and a man standing there asks you, what do you do? And Go! You have 15 seconds to introduce yourself and give a few highlighted facts about yourself. That's literally what it is, a 15 second spiel, about yourself, so be creative talk quickly about your current position, wins, and what your goals are for the near future. This is not easy unless you've done it before, and have it locked down in your mind so it becomes repetitive and memorized. When you're communicating try to avoid words like always, never, etc. These words are "absolute" and convey a meaning of negativity. If I said, "You're always late to meetings." Or you, "Never" come to work on time. The fact is, those statements probably are not true. Even if the person was late, or never comes to work on time, what if the employee in question has been with the company for 20 years? To say, "Never" or "Always" is a generalization of actions. Get your emotions under control, when you speak to people. Reaffirm your faith in the person to do better, define positive steps for them to take and don't forget to give them positive feedback. Everyone you come in contact with will have a diverse work style, so you must develop a sense of self awareness and understand your leadership style. What is your style? Are you a teacher, visionary, healer, warrior? You have the ability to be all of these. You can create a path in your relationship with many approaches. You can be a person of action, assertive, and like to determine the course of events, and think in terms of the bottom line. In your relationship will you be the Leader? Will you delegate responsibility, and give opportunities for others to make decisions? Or will you be more of a hands-off type of person in the relationship? Whatever you decide to be, remember that your contribution is important, and your relationship mindset can help you go further towards your final goal.

CHAPTER

21

Your Money

To MAKE MONEY, YOU have to deliver your energy in some form, you have to be able to satisfy a demand of some sort that is out there already. If what you're selling is charisma, energy, and enthusiasm there is no competition, because most everyone else is selling things that are lifeless and dull. So the things that you are selling must be unique, different and desirable. Why? Because it will excite people and bring them to life. So no matter whatever it is that you are selling make it exciting, make it fun and it will become easy to sell when you put your life into your products. So along with your energy you will see that the law of supply and demand no longer applies. It does not apply once you understand the trick of projecting your energy into the activities that you do and the things that you create. You have to switch your focus from yourself, from what do I need? or what will I eat? to how will I fulfill somebody else's needs today?, and get paid in the process. There is no way of making money other than for filling someone else's needs. First, you concentrate on serving others and in that way you will be able to serve yourself. So what will you supply? People buy services, knowledge, or products. So when people are attracted to what you are, you have to have knowledge, a service or a product to sell them. By concentrating on what people need, you become abundant when we look at the marketplace of life, isn't it true that so many products don't work? How many restaurants have you eaten at and they are not clean or customer oriented? There's so many people that rip off merchants who have not tapped into, How will I fulfill my customers needs? If you're selling a product that you believe in ask yourself, can I put my heart and soul into this product? Can I be enthusiastic and really love this product? Can this really serve my customers? You have to remember that concentrating on people is a form of love. When you stand in the showroom explaining the selling benefits of a car it's an act of love. You're selling this car because in effect you have love for this car and it's very easy for you to talk about something that you love. You can at that point convince another person to love that car too and perhaps buy it from you. You have to join humanity of the level of emotions, needs and understanding you have to nurture people and put out good energy if you expect to sell a product. To sell things successfully, you have to put your ego away long enough to take people's money. This might sound rude but in fact it is not. You have to listen to others, you have to watch their eyes, notice their body language and relate to them, ask them questions, and think to yourself what does this person want? Then give them what they want. Think about how you can improve what you do even if you work for someone else right now, start putting more energy and if you work in a place that is lifeless be the energy that is there and it will catapult you to a better place. You need to offer love, kindness, and energy. When you concentrate on people by providing things for them, you're falling in love with them. Choose love to make your life abundant and in that the love should be unconditional as best as you can manage, never forget that. If you sell information make it clear and concise so everyone can understand you have to think of others. There are loads of people out there who are not very clever, but they have a lot of money. Will they understand what you were offering? Remember that you are a teacher, you're helping people, you're making them feel safer taking them from fear to love from ignorance to knowledge, by mentally pushing these ideas into what you do, you're projecting the light out of yourself and you are offering them light. You never have to compete with anyone once you infuse your products your life or anything that you are selling with love and energy, visualize the energy going into your product right now. Close your eyes and imagine that what you are selling, what you are hoping for are dreaming about is right in front of you inches away from your face and you're destined to receive it. Don't destroy yourself with negative feelings toward other people, if you can't love them be neutral. Be Enthusiastic, be loving, be open but don't limit yourself and don't get stuck in one place or in one salary for the rest of your life, agree to have an action plan. It will carry you higher and you will have a greater velocity, a larger salary and bigger opportunities when it opens up and it is easy money. You will find money, you will win money, a great amount will suddenly and unexpectedly fall into your lap so get ready and expect a huge payout. You've worked hard you've made many sacrifices and you've had many sleepless nights you have challenged yourself for more. If you energize yourself into your work you will find that, the job becomes more fun to do, you'll be more likely to be promoted and given a raise. You left your energy level so high that you'll go beyond the job and perhaps to another corporation that pays you even more. By arriving a little earlier, staying a little later, you increase your efficiency and you can relate better to the people around you. Get out a piece of paper write down the services, knowledge, or products you are familiar with, the things that you are doing, the things that you are interested in delivering to the people and just like that you've created an action plan that will take you further than you can imagine. You will improve your money and you will be surprised at how easy it falls like rain from the sky. Ask yourself, what am I good up at? What do I like to do, that people will pay me for? Are you an Artist? Writer? That inner talent you have, it's time to turn that into cash. People will Pay you for that inner talent, you just have to be creative and promote it. I knew a man who wasn't Educated, he grew up from a poor community, so he didn't have the background or connections to do much. He knew that was good at one thing though. He could sweep, he could clean a window so well, that if you looked at it, you would think it was not there. That's how clean it would look, completely spotless. He started going to businesses and offering them free window cleaning and office cleaning, and if they liked his work, they could pay him the next time around. You would not believe how many businesses would take him up on his offer. He started with one small office, and did very well, cleaning it and the word started to spread. He went from one office to hundreds of offices and he got so busy so fast he had to hire 50 employees he had so much work to do. Now his cleaning business is very successful. As you can imagine he doesn't clean anymore, people clean for him. It started though with him taking the initiative first. He knew he didn't have the education or the background, but he knew what he was good at, and he thought to himself, I've got this inner talent, that I am very good at and if I get creative, I can use this talent to make money and get out of my poor environment. So I ask you again, What are you good at? Don't let your inner talent die inside of you. Expose your talent, and feed it daily. What have you done today to feed that creative monster inside of you. Don't tell me you don't have something you're good at! Can you cook? Make a cookbook and sell it. Can you write? Start a blog on your favorite topic or write a book. One of my hidden talents is that I think I am pretty good cook. Although I don't see myself making a cookbook, I know that my mom could make one, she's got so many recipes of southern dishes that it would be very easy for her to make one, if she ever wanted to. Start to dive into yourself, the possibilities are unlimited. I love the television show, "Shark Tank." The reason why is because that show is made for people with dreams. Creative inventors come and showcase their product to the panel in hopes of getting an investment on their idea. Some win over the panel and some do not, but either way just to make it on the show itself, gets you national exposure, no matter if the panel likes your idea or not. There are many other people with money in the world that may just love your product and invest more into you and your idea than they ever could. You have to be willing to expand your thought process. Don't think, this is it. This is my only shot, and if I don't make it I never will. The world is full of people that will love your idea! Your attitude should be, someone is going to love my idea, someone is going to love my product! Millions are going to buy my product! Invoke, Invoke, Invoke! You have to speak your money into existence! I don't care if you don't have two nickels to rub together at the moment, and your bank account is overdrawn. Don't talk about that lack, talk about what's coming, what you're going to have, until you get it. Push out the positive talk first and foremost. As I am writing, my body is trying to tell me, I am getting a cold, so I started taking some Dayquil, people have come in my office and asked, "Are you getting sick?" I say, "No I feel great, I am not sick at all." I am claiming what I know to be true. If I say otherwise, my body and mind will only intensify a sick, defeated feeling. I don't want that, do you? I am speaking health into my life, I am speaking wellness into my life, even though my nose, and throat are trying to say something else. I won't admit that I am sick, even if I might feel that way. My wife has a tendency of asking me how she looks, and even if I know she is very tired from being with the kids all day long, I will say, "You look fine." She knows she won't get a defeated answer out of me. She knows I won't say, "Wow, you look so tired." She knows I don't want to make it worse by spreading negativity. It does no one any good to speak like that. We should be encouraging one another, not bringing them down. It works in all aspects of life, you can speak the blessings over, your money, spouse, children, whomever. I can't tell you how many times you can say something to a person and instantly they feel better. Maybe they were worried about something they were going through, and you came along and said that one thing that made them feel better. The power is in your tongue. You can use it to improve anything, use it wisely!

CHAPTER

The Great Divide

You will start to see success, but how you treat your new found glory will be your indication if you can keep it long enough to enjoy it. Hopefully by now you have built a strong solid team of positive individuals that you can trust. You will need separation between what you used to do and what you currently do now. I call this the "Great Divide." Once you start being successful, recognize that you are not the same. You cannot be at the same places, be seen so much, or talk the same way. There is a saying that says, "A man with money, has no time, and a man with time, has no money." You cannot be all things to all people. When you really start working on yourself, your ideas, or project, you don't have time to waste. You can't be out at every party, club or social event. Those things will not help you achieve anything. You have to decide what you really want. Do you want to hang out all night drinking with the same old people? Or would you rather spend your time working on your future? It takes a mature person to say, "I'd rather focus on myself, than going to that party." It's very hard especially when you're young to turn down, all the things you'd rather do. However it becomes easy to do, when you have a plan and know exactly what you want to do. People will treat you differently, they will notice you are different. They will notice the inner confidence you have in your abilities, and it will shine through the way you carry yourself. Some will adapt to it and some will fall out of touch with you, and that is fine. The people that are meant to be in your life, will never leave you. Some people are only supposed to be with you only for a season, and just like leaves they will fall away from you. You wondered why your relationship didn't last? It wasn't supposed to. Everything that has happened in your life has a purpose, the good and the bad. It may not be easy to believe, but everything that you've been through is something that you can teach someone else that is going through the exact same thing. I would never want to make light of very serious or dangerous things that might have happened to you. But can I tell you, you're still here, you're still standing strong, and because you are, your life is a testimony and you can be a huge blessing to someone in the same situation you went through. Turn it all around. The pain and sorrow you experienced someone else has too. You can teach someone how to divide that pain and use that energy to help someone. Dividing the negative thoughts and people from your life is very important in order to move forward. I love the definition of the word, "Divide" it means to separate or be separated into parts. There are many things you need to separate, yourself from in order to be where you want in life. I used to know a lady who loved her husband very much, but he was always in trouble, in and out of jail, on drugs, always in trouble with the law. Even though he was a bad man, she loved him with all her heart and tried over and over to talk to him, make things right and be a family. But the reality was, he was too weak, and was not going to change. I told her, what I am telling you to do, you must separate yourself from those influences. Yes it may be hard, but what is more important? Their life? Or yours? You have to do things to protect yourself and your family first. You need some division in your life in order to reach your true potential. You can't be buddy, buddy with everyone, because, they don't have your best interest at heart. I have seen so many people try to make everyone their friend. They care so much about what other people think and do, that they forget what they are supposed to be concerned with, themselves. You have to stop worrying about what other people think, your dreams are your own. I've seen many go through a bitter divorce just to start a new relationship and then carry all the mistakes over to the new spouse, trying to make the new person pay. Don't punish the new person you're married to now, for things that happened years ago, that's not fair. They can't pay you back, let it go. If you are willing to do this you will come out better than before. You may feel guilty about something that wasn't even your fault. Don't feel bad, instead hold your head up high. Your value doesn't go down, because someone mistreated you. Not everyone can go where, your destiny is taking you. I am strong believer that God, will be your great divider, he will replace the negative people in your life with positive ones. The scriptures say weeping may endure for a night, but joy comes in the morning. That to me simply means that the pain, the struggle the lack is only temporary, and God will bring you out better than you were before. Your future is too big to reach on your own. God has already arranged the right people at the right time to come into your life and give you exactly what you need. Will you trust him? Some people never get to where they are supposed to be, or reach their highest potential because they never get away from the wrong people. Your path should be filled with people, who challenge you, who motivate you. You should not hear a yes, every time you make a suggestion, you need to have thinkers and doers around you all the time. Connect with people, who understand your uniqueness, your plans, and those that encourage you. Divide yourself from anyone, who is trying to set you back. This is your season to connect with the right people. Run your own race, and don't worry about what other people are doing. I have seen too many people in business so focused on what the competition is doing that they end up losing everything. You can only do the best you can do, so quit thinking that you have to measure up to everyone else. You're in a class all by yourself. Be comfortable in your own skin and know that you are loved. You don't have to win people over or buy their love. I've seen people go out of their way trying to buy peoples affection, and that never works. If someone likes you, they will like you, no matter if you're rich or poor, give them gifts or nothing at all. You have something great to offer people. Your smile, your friendship, your personality, your conversation. It may be easy for you to see how great everyone else is, but never forget the greatness within you. There is nothing wrong with looking up to people, we all should have a mentor, someone that we can talk to and look to for life advice. But don't give up your identity for theirs, run your own race, be your own person, and divide yourself from the negatives. Know what you are and what you're not. You must understand your limits. You cannot drive a Jeep the same way you would drive a Corvette. A Corvette is a sports car, designed to accelerate fast and be driven fast, while the Jeep knows that it cannot accelerate at a Corvettes pace, it wasn't designed to be a sports car, it's knows it's limits. Each car, just like each person is designed with a specific purpose. You were not created to compare your life with someone else's. Having those feelings will only create a constant struggle within yourself. I know ladies who are size 1 and ladies who are size 21, and can I tell you there is no difference between them. Why? No matter their size they strut around and know how to accessorize what they have and use what God Blessed them with to the fullest. They are not in competition because they know their worth, their value. It's that confidence they have within them, that draws the best things toward them. So when you meet a woman like that, you can't help but think, "She's got it going on." You have to be confident and happy, and that will make you stand out from the rest. I have interviewed thousands of people and hired a few hundred. The people that I hire are the people that stood out the most, came in with their heads held high and had so much confidence in themselves and their ability I would often hire them on the spot. They knew how to sell themselves, how to show off their inner greatness, without overly doing it. They knew what to say and when to say it. They knew how they should dress and act in the interview. I have also seen the opposite people that come in not dressed appropriately and expect to get to get hired, never forget your appearance is how people will remember you, so be sharp. Always show up to work. I have seen too many people terminated because they couldn't divide the party lifestyle from work responsibilities. You must be able to separate yourself from what you want to do, to what you know you should be doing. Everything that happens to you from this moment forward take ownership of it! The successes and the failures, because that is what is developing you for greatness. I know you've made some bad decisions, who hasn't? Learn and grow from it.

CHAPTER

23

No Apologies Needed

You don't ever have to feel bad about being successful. You set a goal and you accomplished it! You wanted to lose weight or get in better shape and you did. Don't let someone who doesn't get off the couch make you feel bad. Always wear your blessings well. Too many times you might feel like, since you got a new car, a promotion or something good has happened that you must shrink back, and act like nothing happened. We should be doing the opposite, we should be bragging on the Goodness of God! When something spectacular happens, say "Look at God." It shows you recognize where it all came from, and you open up room for more. Don't apologize or feel sorry for all the goodness that is coming your way. Receive it and be ready for more. Wear a smile as often as you can.

We all know people with the same old face, they never smile, just a straight face all the time. Their life reflects their face. If they have no joy, you can see it on their face, and the opposite is true. When you are happy, you feel good, and it rubs off on other people, even the mean ones. Simply give credit where credit is due, to the most high. All through the day praise God and praise his goodness. Never apologize or try to downplay God's goodness or he will find somebody else to favor. If he did it for you he can do it for someone else as well. If you are the kind of person that always sees promotion, healing, good opportunities coming your way just recognize that as a gift from God and don't have any problem wearing that blessing well. I used to feel guilty when I looked at my life and compared it to some of my friends that I grew up with or high school friends. Sometimes I would try to downplay what God has blessed me with so that I would not make others feel bad, but then I learned that does not bring any praise or honor to God. God wants us to be an example of his goodness and I learned I don't have to apologize if I get a load of new blessings and someone else doesn't. I give God the credit, all of it 100%. I have nothing without him. Doors that no man can shut. When doors open and you move into that new home or new job for the promotion that you have been praying for others may be mad. They may be negative or critical but don't allow those people to try to bring you down to their level what is meant for you will be for you and what is made for them will be from them. If you want to be in alignment with God and live in happiness enjoy life you cannot be defeated, depressed or have a broken attitude. Stop apologizing to people that don't matter, and wear your blessings well and enjoy God's favor. Be proud of what God has done in your life but make sure you always give him the credit. You did nothing on your own, you did everything with his help. You never have to hide your passion, hide your happiness, hide your victory or your possessions. You don't have to look poor, dress poor, act poor, or think poor to show people that you're humble. Your humbleness will show through when you give credit to God and not yourself. Some people will tell you not to be so happy but let that go in one ear and out the other you continue to be happy, and you continue to run your race and remember to give God the glory. Be proud of who you are and everything he has done in your life. Sometimes we think so small. We limit ourselves but never forget that God owns it all, the earth, the universe and everything in it is his. We need to enlarge our vision we need to think bigger and use the unlimited potential that he has given you. If you don't step up and wear your attitude well, and where your blessing well, do you know what will happen? It could be given to someone else! Don't worry if people are jealous of you or turn against you or feel that you should not be so blessed. I've learned that some people will only be your friend until you get promoted. Coworkers may go to lunch with you as long as you are on the same level but the moment you were promoted the moment the blessing comes upon you they will try to make you look bad but don't worry about it that Time will take care of all of your enemies. A long time ago I had a Supervisor who did everything in his power to make me look bad. He couldn't stand to see the other co-workers liked me better than him, and would come talk to me before him, it made him so mad he tried to get me fired. What he failed to realize was that he was a very negative person, and no one wanted to be around him. A short time later I was promoted to better position, and he continued to work and be miserable every day of his life. The lesson is be grateful for the goodness that he is put into your life. Our attitude should not be look at all the things I have done look at how big I am no it should be the opposite look at how great God is look at what the Lord has done in your life. All through the day we should be bragging on the goodness of God. You can do this. Starting now and every day going forward you can change your life. You can focus on positive solutions and have a positive attitude. You can surround yourself with supportive people to rise above all of the negativity. You can put your faith in God and trust that he has the best plan for your future. You can be happy who God made you to be and enjoy each day of life and recognize that it is a gift from him. You can forgive others, those people who have done wrong to you. You can help others achieve their goals and dreams. You can be faithful in a relationship. You can be a healer to someone who is hurting. You can be honest with someone who needs a listening ear. You can spread love and happiness to everyone that you come in contact with. You can make your life more amazing than it has already been. You can be the difference maker not only in your life but in the lives of others around you. The reality is you can become anything you want as I stated earlier the power is within you and I believe your destiny is greater than you know. My question to you is what are you going do about it once you finish reading this book? What are you going to do that is going to change your world and make this one a better place? You have been believing, you have been hoping, you have been planning, it's time to take action You can, End of Story, Now You Can Unleash Your Power Within!

Printed in the United States
By Bookmasters